Faith-i-tude:

Believe it. Speak it. Watch God Do It.

100 Days of Believing God For The Impossible—Every Single Day.

Dr. Unnia L. Pettus, Ph.D.

Published By: Nobody But God Ministries Publishing

Library of Congress Cataloging-in-Publication Data has been applied for
ISBN: 979-8-9939712-0-9

PRINTED IN THE UNITED STATES OF AMERICA

Dedication

To every survivor, dreamer, and believer who has ever whispered, "Lord, I still believe."

This book is for you—the ones who have fought battles seen and unseen and still carry the fragrance of faith. May every page remind you that God still works miracles and that your tears have never been wasted.

Acknowledgments

I thank God first—for life, healing, and every breath that fuels my purpose.

To my mother, Ms. Beverly N. Hudgens, family, friends, and prayer warriors who believed even when I was tired: thank you for standing in the gap.

To the pastors, mentors, and congregations who have welcomed my voice into pulpits across the world, thank you for affirming the call of God on my life.

To every survivor reading these words—of sickness, heartbreak, trauma, or tragedy—know this: we overcome by the blood of the Lamb and the word of our testimony. Your faith-i-tude is not arrogance; it's evidence that God still reigns.

Table of Contents

Introduction

WHAT IS FAITH~I~TUDE?

Faith-i-tude is a word God gave me in the fire. It's how I made it through four cancer diagnoses, heart failure, and a stroke that left my right side paralyzed — and how I still speak, write, walk, and serve today.

It's not a catchphrase.

It's a survival strategy.

It's a spiritual mindset.

It's a choice to stand strong on what you believe, even when everything you feel says give up.

Faith-i-tude (noun): A bold, unshakable mindset rooted in unwavering belief in God's promises — especially in moments of testing, trauma, or transition. It is the attitude of someone whose faith speaks louder than their fear, pain, or doubt.

The Greek word for faith is "pistis" — meaning trust, belief, confidence, and conviction. It's not passive. It's active trust in God based on what you know of His character, not what you see in your circumstances.

The Hebrew word for faith is "emunah" — meaning firmness, steadiness, moral fidelity, and truth. Not just "I believe," but, "I'm standing firm no matter what."

Put these together, and you get the heart of Faith-i-tude: A firm, steady, deeply rooted trust in God that doesn't fold under pressure. I also want you to understand that Faith-i-tude is a universal concept, applicable to the lives of believers and those of other faiths. It is also a concept for those who may not be religious or spiritual but want a perspective to tackle life's challenges with courage and positivity rather than doom and gloom. It starts with how you think, which then leads to how you act.

THE BIRTH OF FAITH-I-TUDE

There are moments when faith becomes more than a word. It becomes oxygen. After facing multiple cancers, surviving a stroke, domestic violence, and countless nights of uncertainty, I discovered something powerful—faith isn't passive. It's a posture. God whispered to my heart one day: "You don't just have faith, Unnia—you've got Faith-i-tude." That word became the anthem of my comeback.

Faith-i-tude means having a faith so fierce that it refuses to flinch in the face of fear. It's the audacity to believe when nothing makes sense. It's the courage to keep worshipping while waiting. It's what made Noah build, Abraham trust, Esther risk, and Mary say yes.

This 100-day devotional was birthed out of pain and transformed into purpose. It's designed to cultivate in you the same spiritual boldness that caused me to get up again when life tried to bury me. Each day invites you to read, reflect, write, and rise—stronger, braver, and more faith-filled than before.

So, wherever you are—morning coffee, midnight tears, or a lunch break prayer—let every page pull you closer to the God who makes impossible things possible.

WHY THIS BOOK, AND WHY NOW?

Because people are breaking. People are burning out. People are holding on with tired hands and trembling hearts. And many are asking quietly, "Can I still believe God — even after this?" Maybe you've been there. Maybe you're there right now. You've smiled through grief. You've worked through weakness. You've prayed through pain. You've shown up while silently bleeding. You haven't given up — but you're worn down.

Faith-i-tude is for those of us who love God deeply but are in a season where our faith needs refreshing, refueling, and a reset.

MY WHY

I didn't write this book from a place of theory. I wrote it from the hospital bed. From the chemo chair.

From the prayer closet. From the broken places where I met God in ways I never expected. There were nights I couldn't walk. Days I couldn't speak. Moments I wondered if my life still mattered. But even in the silence, God was speaking. Even when I was still, He was still sovereign. And even when I couldn't lift my hands, my heart was lifted by grace. I survived because God sustained me. I healed because faith held me. I kept going because I had a faith-i-tude — and I want to help you build yours, too.

WHAT TO EXPECT

Each chapter of this book is a blend of:
- Bible teaching with Hebrew and Greek word studies
- Faith coaching from someone who's walked through storms
- Reflection space and personal journal moments
- Faith-in-action strategies that stretch your mindset
- You'll meet real people from the Bible who had to fight for faith:
- Job, who worshiped with wounds
- Hannah, who prayed through pain
- The bleeding woman, who pressed forward despite shame
- Paul, who wrote letters from prison
- Mary, who carried a promise that didn't make sense

This book is for the one who's still standing — even if you're standing on a shaky leg and a whispered prayer.

HOW TO USE THIS 100-DAY DEVOTIONAL AND JOURNAL

1. Read the Scripture Slowly. Let the Word soak into your spirit before reading the reflection.

2. Meditate on the Message. Allow each devotional to speak to where you are right now.

3. Write Your Reflections. Use the lined spaces after each devotional to capture what God reveals.

4. Pray Boldly. Don't rush through the closing prayer—pray it aloud.

Declare Daily. At the end of each devotional, you'll find "My Faith Notes for Today" and "My Faith Declaration." Speak these aloud. Faith grows when it's expressed.

A FINAL WORD BEFORE WE BEGIN

Let me speak to your spirit:
- You are not too broken to be used.
- You are not too tired to believe again.

- You are not forgotten, overlooked, or disqualified.
- You are in the middle of becoming.
- God is still building you.

Faith-i-tude is your reminder that breakthrough is not just possible — it's personal.

Take a breath. Turn the page. Let's walk this out together — one act of faith at a time.

Days 1 ~ 10:
Faith That Sees

Day 1
Faith That Sees the Invisible
— Hebrews 11:1 —
Abraham, Noah, Joseph, David, Sarah

"Now faith is the substance of things hoped for, the evidence of things not seen."
— Hebrews 11: 1 (KJV)

DEVOTIONAL

Faith begins where sight ends. To see the invisible is to believe beyond what your eyes report and to trust what your spirit knows. Abraham had this kind of faith when God told him to look toward heaven and count the stars. Noah had it when he built an ark while the sun was still shining. This seeing-without-seeing faith moves mountains because it starts with believing that God's word outweighs human evidence.

When God speaks, faith invites you to imagine what doesn't exist yet. That's why visionaries often walk alone for a season; their faith paints pictures others can't see. Joseph saw himself ruling while he was still wearing a shepherd's robe. David saw victory before he picked up the stone. Visionary faith isn't blind optimism—it's divine perception. It looks at chaos and sees creation waiting to be commanded.

If you've ever been misunderstood for dreaming too big, you're in good company. Visionary faith will always look ridiculous to those who only trust what they can touch. Peter looked ridiculous stepping out on water. Sarah looked foolish buying baby clothes at ninety. Yet the God who calls things that are not as though they were specializes in transforming the unseen into the undeniable.

Perhaps you're staring at an empty bank account, a doctor's report, or a delayed promise. Visionary faith doesn't deny the facts; it declares a higher truth: "With God all things are possible." (Matthew 19 : 26 NIV) The facts say "impossible," but faith whispers, "inevitable." Every delay is God's opportunity to demonstrate His divine timing.

To cultivate this faith, you must feed your vision with the Word daily. What you repeatedly hear shapes what you believe. When fear says, "give up," faith says, "look up." Faith doesn't need full details; it just needs one word from God. Abraham left his homeland "not knowing whither he went." (Hebrews 11 : 8 KJV) The journey of faith always starts with an unclear map but a clear promise.

Ask yourself: What dream has God placed in my spirit that still feels too distant? What invisible thing am I called to believe into being? Visionary faith invites you to partner with God's imagination—to build, write, forgive, or launch before it makes sense.

When you can't see the finish line, hold on to the voice that called you to start. The invisible today will be undeniable tomorrow.

REFLECTIVE STANCE:
How can I train my spiritual eyes to see what God is doing before it manifests?

____

____

____

"Faith isn't pretending not to see reality—it's choosing to see God's promise as more real than the problem."
— Rev. Unnia L. Pettus, Ph.D.

PRAYER:
Lord, thank You for the gift of vision that transcends sight. Help me to trust You when I can't trace You. Teach me to walk by faith, not by fear, and to declare Your promises over what appears impossible. Give me eyes to see hope in dark places and courage to keep moving when the path is unclear. Renew my mind so I focus on Your unseen hand at work. Strengthen my belief until my faith becomes sight. In Jesus's name, Amen.

MY FAITH NOTES FOR TODAY

____

____

____

MY FAITH DECLARATION:

I see beyond what is and believe in what God has promised.

____

____

____

DAY 2
Faith That Walks Without a Map
— Hebrews 11:8 —
Abraham

"By faith Abraham, when he was called to go out into a place which he should after receive for an inheritance, obeyed; and he went out, not knowing whither he went."
— Hebrews 11 : 8 (KJV)

DEVOTIONAL

Faith is seldom comfortable. The call of God almost always pulls us out of what is familiar into what is forming. Abraham's story shows that obedience often begins with uncertainty. When God told him to leave his homeland, He didn't hand him a GPS or a five-year plan. He gave him a word and a promise. Faith says yes when comfort says no. The moment you agree with God's command, heaven begins rearranging earth to make room for your obedience.

Leaving your comfort zone does not mean abandoning wisdom; it means trusting divine direction above human calculation. Every destiny requires displacement. Noah had to step out of normality to build something the world had never seen. Moses had to leave the palace to find his purpose in the wilderness. Ruth had to leave Moab to step into Bethlehem's blessing. God never calls us out without preparing a place to bring us in.

Fear will always whisper, "What if you fail?" but faith answers, "What if I fly?" Comfort creates complacency; calling creates courage. There is a moment when you must decide that staying where you are costs more than stepping where God is calling you. The disciples left their nets because a greater catch awaited them in the sea of souls. When you cling to safety, you sacrifice destiny.

Perhaps you feel stuck between "what was" and "what will be." Faith flourishes in that in-between place. God is not asking you to understand every detail—He's asking you to trust every direction. Each act of obedience opens another door. Abraham didn't see Canaan in one leap; he saw it step by step. Faith develops by movement, not management.

The comfort zone feels secure, but it limits growth. A seed never fulfills its purpose until it's buried. Likewise, faith grows when it is planted in unfamiliar soil. When you dare to go where God sends you, He provides provision, protection, and peace for the journey. Sometimes you must walk away from good to receive God's best.

If God is stirring something new in you—an idea, ministry, relationship, or mission—don't fight the stretching. Stretching precedes strengthening. The same God who called you out will walk beside you all the way. Every step of obedience is a declaration: "Lord, I trust You more than I trust my comfort."

Leaving your comfort zone is not a one-time event; it's a lifestyle of faith. Each new level of glory demands another leap. The good news is that you never jump alone. God catches, carries, and completes every willing heart that dares to move when He says go.

REFLECTIVE STANCE:

Where is God asking me to step out in faith today?

____

____

____

"Faith isn't brave because it's fearless—it's brave because it moves while still trembling."

— Rev. Unnia L. Pettus, Ph.D.

PRAYER:

Lord, thank You for calling me beyond what feels safe. Give me courage to follow where You lead, even when I don't have all the answers. Teach me to release fear and embrace faith, to trade certainty for trust. Let my obedience open doors that fear once closed. Strengthen my steps and silence my doubts. Remind me that wherever You guide, You also provide. I choose movement over mediocrity and destiny over comfort. In Jesus's name, Amen.

MY FAITH NOTES FOR TODAY

____

____

____

MY FAITH DECLARATION:

I will step out in faith, trusting that God has already gone before me.

____

____

____

DAY 3
Faith That Waits Well
— Isaiah 40:31 —
Hannah, Simeon, Anna

"My sheep hear my voice, and I know them, and they follow me."
— John 10 : 27 (KJV)

DEVOTIONAL

Hearing God's voice is the heartbeat of faith. True faith is not just believing God exists—it's following His direction even when others don't hear what you hear. From Genesis to Revelation, every great move of God started with a word. Noah built an ark because he heard. Moses confronted Pharaoh because he heard. Mary carried the Messiah because she heard. To follow His voice is to anchor your life to divine instruction, not public opinion.

The challenge is that God rarely speaks in the thunder; He whispers in the stillness. Elijah discovered this on Mount Horeb when the Lord was not in the wind, the earthquake, or the fire but in the gentle whisper. Faith trains the ear to recognize that whisper amid the noise of fear, culture, and distraction. The

Shepherd's voice never contradicts His Word; it confirms it. When you live tuned to His frequency, you stop reacting to chaos and start responding to clarity.

Following God's voice often requires going against the crowd. Noah was mocked. Abraham left familiarity. Peter stepped out of the boat while others stayed behind. God's directions may seem illogical because they lead to supernatural outcomes. When He said to Israel, "March around the walls," He was preparing victory through obedience, not strategy. Faith listens when logic balks.

Maybe you're asking, "Lord, is that You or my own thoughts?" The more time you spend in His presence, the clearer His tone becomes. His voice carries peace, never panic; conviction, never condemnation. When you recognize His rhythm, you walk with divine confidence. The enemy mimics noise, but he cannot counterfeit peace.

God's voice will always lead you toward purpose. When He told Philip to leave revival in Samaria for one Ethiopian soul, that simple obedience advanced the gospel to Africa. One whisper changed continents. Your yes to God's prompting can shift generations. Following His voice may seem small now, but it echoes eternally.

Faith that follows hears with the heart before the ears. It says, "Speak, Lord, for Your servant hears." When you obey quickly, heaven responds powerfully. Every miracle is born in a moment of obedience. The same voice that calmed the sea still speaks calm to your storms today

REFLECTIVE STANCE:
How can I quiet distractions to better hear and obey God's voice?

____

____

____

"Faith grows in the silence where God's whisper becomes louder than the world's noise."

— Rev. Unnia L. Pettus, Ph.D.

PRAYER:
Father, thank You for speaking to me. Help me to discern Your voice above every competing sound. Teach me to listen with humility, obey with courage, and walk with peace. When You speak, give me faith to follow even when I don't see the full picture. Let Your Word light my path and guard my steps. Tune my spirit to Your frequency and silence every false echo. I desire not just to hear You but to follow You fully. In Jesus's name, Amen.

MY FAITH NOTES FOR TODAY

MY FAITH DECLARATION:
I will follow God's voice with confidence, knowing His direction leads to destiny.

DAY 4
Faith That Speaks to Mountains
— Mark 11:23 —
Jesus and the Disciples

"And he arose, and rebuked the wind, and said unto the sea, Peace, be still. And the wind ceased, and there was a great calm."
— Mark 4 : 39 (KJV)

DEVOTIONAL

Storms are not proof that God has left; they are classrooms where He teaches trust. When the disciples found themselves tossed by wind and waves, they panicked, forgetting the One sleeping in their boat. Jesus never promised life without storms; He promised presence within them. Faith that stands in the storm doesn't deny the danger—it decides that peace is possible in the middle of it.

Every believer encounters seasons when the winds howl louder than the promises. Bills pile, friends fade, prayers feel unanswered. Yet the same Jesus who silenced Galilee's waters still speaks to modern chaos. The secret is not the absence of the storm but the awareness of the Savior. When fear shouts, faith whispers, "He's still in the boat."

Storms test what we believe about God. Anyone can worship on calm seas, but real faith anchors when waves rise. Job lost everything and still declared, "Though he slay me, yet will I trust in him." (Job 13:15 KJV) Paul sang in prison at midnight. Their circumstances didn't change before their confession did. Faith learns to speak peace before peace appears.

Sometimes God calms the storm; sometimes He calms the sailor. When He said "Peace, be still," He wasn't only talking to the sea—He was talking to the souls in the boat. Faith holds fast not because it understands, but because it remembers. The same God who brought you through the last storm is capable of bringing you through this one.

Standing in the storm requires perspective. What looks like punishment may be preparation. The tempest that terrified the disciples trained them for ministry. Every crash of thunder reminded them of His authority. You cannot discover the power of His word until you've seen what His word can silence.

If your world feels shaken, grab hold of the Word. Declare, "Peace, be still," over your home, health, or heart. Faith does not focus on the storm's size but on the Savior's sovereignty. Even if the boat rocks, your belief doesn't have to. Storms end, but the strength gained from surviving them remains.

When the clouds clear, you'll realize you were never sinking—you were being steered. Storm faith is steady faith; it refuses to drown where Jesus dwells.

REFLECTIVE STANCE:
Where in my life do I need to speak "Peace, be still?"

____

____

____

"Faith doesn't wait for the storm to pass; it learns to rest while the wind still blows."
— Rev. Unnia L. Pettus, Ph.D.

PRAYER:
Lord, thank You for being my shelter in every storm. Teach me to trust Your presence more than I fear the waves. When anxiety rises, remind me that You command both wind and water. Speak peace to my troubled heart and stillness to my restless mind. Help me to remember past deliverances so I stand firm in present trials. Let my life testify that storms reveal, not remove, Your power. In Jesus's name, Amen.

MY FAITH NOTES FOR TODAY

____

____

____

MY FAITH DECLARATION:

I will stand firm in every storm, knowing Jesus is in my boat.

____

____

____

DAY 5
Faith That Rises From the Ruins
— Nehemiah 2:17–20 —
Nehemiah

"But they that wait upon the Lord shall renew their strength; they shall mount up with wings as eagles; they shall run, and not be weary; and they shall walk, and not faint."
— Isaiah 40: 31 (KJV)

DEVOTIONAL

Waiting is one of faith's hardest disciplines. We live in a culture of instant downloads, but God develops destiny in delays. While we rush, He refines. Faith to wait well means trusting that divine timing is not denial. Abraham waited twenty-five years for Isaac, Joseph thirteen years for his dream, and Jesus thirty years before His public ministry. Delay is not defeat; it's development.

Waiting well is active, not idle. It doesn't mean sitting in despair; it means serving while expecting. David tended sheep while waiting to be king. Hannah kept praying while barren. Simeon worshiped daily until he held the Messiah. Waiting is the proving ground of worship. If you can praise in a pause, you're ready for promotion.

Faithful waiting refocuses the heart from the calendar to the Creator. When impatience whispers, "It's taking too long," faith responds, "He's taking His time." Isaiah's promise reminds us that strength is renewed—not drained—when we wait correctly. Those who rush often crash; those who rest in Him rise.

God uses waiting to align us with His will. Some doors remain closed because premature entry would crush us. A butterfly that forces its way out of the cocoon too early can't fly. Likewise, faith trusts the process of preparation. Every "not yet" from heaven protects your "right now" purpose.

The enemy uses waiting seasons to whisper lies: "God forgot you," "Others are ahead of you," "You missed it." But faith counters with truth: "The vision is yet for an appointed time." (Habakkuk 2 : 3 KJV) Faith chooses patience over panic, peace over pressure.

If you're in a holding pattern, remember: wings are strengthened in the wind. Eagles soar only after waiting for the right current. Your time will come when conditions align with your calling. God's timing never arrives late; it always lands ready.

Waiting well is worshiping while watching. Keep believing. Keep building. When He says "now," the wait will make sense, and the strength you've gained will carry you higher than you imagined.

REFLECTIVE STANCE:
How can I honor God during my waiting season?

____

____

____

"Waiting is not wasted when your faith is still working."
— Rev. Unnia L. Pettus, Ph.D.

PRAYER:
Lord, thank You for the patience that perfects me. Help me to trust Your timing when mine runs out. Teach me to worship while I wait and to find purpose in every pause. Renew my strength like the eagle's; lift me above discouragement and delay. Guard me from comparison and keep my heart content in You. May my waiting produce wisdom, maturity, and gratitude. When the appointed time arrives, let me soar by Your Spirit. In Jesus's name, Amen.

MY FAITH NOTES FOR TODAY

MY FAITH DECLARATION:

I will wait with hope, knowing God's delay is preparation, not denial.

DAY 6
Faith That Dares to Dream Again
— Genesis 37:5–11 —
Joseph

"Rejoice not against me, O mine enemy: when I fall, I shall arise; when I sit in darkness, the Lord shall be a light unto me."
— Micah 7:8 (KJV)

DEVOTIONAL

Falling is not final when faith still breathes. Every believer has faced moments when the weight of disappointment seemed too heavy to lift. Yet the very definition of redemption is God's power to raise what has fallen. Faith to rise again does not come from denying the pain—it comes from discovering God's purpose within it.

Peter wept bitterly after denying Christ, but that same Peter preached boldly on Pentecost. Failure was not the finale of his story; it became the foundation for his calling. God specializes in recycling regret into revival. You cannot rise in your own strength, but you can stand again in His grace.

When life knocks you down, the enemy expects you to stay there. He underestimates resurrection power. The same Spirit that raised Jesus from the grave dwells in you. (Romans 8:11 NIV) Every setback is a setup for a stronger comeback. Faith doesn't erase the fall; it transforms it into fuel.

Sometimes the hardest part of rising again is forgiving yourself. Shame whispers, "You blew it." But mercy answers, "You're still chosen." God never consults your past to determine your potential. David wrote psalms after moral failure. Jonah preached revival after rebellion. Your stumble is not stronger than His salvation.

To rise again requires remembering who you are in Christ. The prodigal son rehearsed his repentance speech, yet his father ran to embrace him before he could finish it. Grace outruns guilt every time. Stand up, dust off, and step forward. Heaven rejoices over those who return.

Resurrection faith refuses to quit. It looks at the grave and sees glory. It believes that what looks finished is only forming. Even ashes can't cancel anointing. Faith to rise again means trusting that the light of God still shines in your darkest chapters.
Get up, beloved. The story isn't over. Every scar becomes a sermon. Every tear becomes testimony. When you rise again, you remind hell that grace still wins.

REFLECTIVE STANCE:
What area of my life is God calling me to rise again?

____

____

____

"Falling is human, but rising again is holy."
— Rev. Unnia L. Pettus, Ph.D.

PRAYER:
Lord, thank You for lifting me when I fall. Heal the places in me that have grown weary from failure and fear. Restore my confidence in Your forgiveness. Give me courage to rise again with new strength and fresh purpose. Let Your light break through every shadow and guide me back to the path You designed. Use my scars as signs of Your grace. I declare that I am not finished—I am being formed. In Jesus's name, Amen.

MY FAITH NOTES FOR TODAY

____

____

____

MY FAITH DECLARATION:

I will rise again by the power of God's grace.

____

____

____

DAY 7
Faith That Rebuilds Broken Places
— Isaiah 61:4 —
Ezra, Nehemiah

"Let us not be weary in well doing: for in due season we shall reap, if we faint not."
— Galatians 6:9 (KJV)

DEVOTIONAL

Perseverance is the language of heaven. Faith that refuses to give up is faith that understands timing. We live in an instant world, but God works through process. When you feel tempted to quit, remember that the harvest always hides beneath the soil. Seeds don't shout when they grow—they simply stretch in silence.

Noah hammered nails for decades before he saw a drop of rain. Sarah waited years before laughter filled her tent. Paul kept preaching despite prison and persecution. Every person who accomplished something divine had a moment when quitting looked easier. The difference between them and others wasn't talent—it was tenacity.

Faithful endurance transforms adversity into advancement. Each trial strengthens the muscle of perseverance. James 1:3 (NIV) reminds us, "The testing of your faith produces perseverance." You can't pray for strength and despise the weight that builds it. God doesn't send hardship to break you but to build you.

When fatigue whispers, "Why bother?" remember Galatians 6:9 — your due season is coming. Heaven keeps perfect calendars. What feels delayed on earth is right on schedule in glory. Your assignment is to stay faithful until fulfillment arrives.

Sometimes refusing to give up means redefining progress. Maybe you're not sprinting, but you're still standing—and that's victory. Crawl if you must, but don't stop. Even Jesus carried His cross step by painful step. The crown comes after the climb.

Persevering faith is not loud; it's loyal. It shows up to serve, pray, give, and love when nobody notices. God counts unseen faithfulness as success. The same hand that planted you will reward you.

Keep going. You are closer than you think. Heaven has never lost track of a persistent believer.

REFLECTIVE STANCE:

Where have I been tempted to quit when God is calling me to keep going?

____

____

____

"Persistence turns pain into progress;
endurance turns waiting into winning. "
— Rev. Unnia L. Pettus, Ph.D.

PRAYER:

Lord, strengthen me to finish what You've started in me. Remind me that the reward belongs to the relentless. When I feel weary, renew my spirit and restore my focus. Silence the lies that say it's over and amplify Your promise that it's worth it. Let perseverance produce character and hope within me. Help me to walk by faith when results seem far away. Thank You that my due season is already on the calendar of heaven. In Jesus's name, Amen.

MY FAITH NOTES FOR TODAY

____

____

____

MY FAITH DECLARATION:

I will not quit; I will reap because I refuse to faint.

____

____

____

DAY 8
Faith That Starts Small
— Matthew 17:20 —
Jesus' Teaching on the Mustard Seed

"Jesus said unto him, If thou canst believe, all things are possible to him that believeth."
— Mark 9 : 23 (KJV)

DEVOTIONAL

There comes a time when faith must be rekindled after disappointment. The father who cried, "Lord, I believe; help thou mine unbelief," (Mark 9 : 24) speaks for many hearts. Believing again after heartbreak is one of the bravest acts a soul can perform.

Doubt is not the opposite of faith; giving up is. The very fact that you are wrestling means you still care. Thomas doubted until he touched the scars, yet Jesus didn't condemn him—He invited him closer. The Lord meets us in our questions, not away from them.

Believing again means confronting memories of unmet expectations. Maybe you prayed for healing that didn't come, or a door that never opened. Faith doesn't pretend those moments didn't hurt—it chooses to trust again despite them. Resurrection always happens after crucifixion.

When Jesus visited the tomb of Lazarus, He asked Martha, "Do you believe?" Faith had to override grief. When you believe again, you declare that loss cannot have the last word. Every "no" you've heard from life is still subject to God's greater "yes."

Believing again is also about the restoration of joy. Hope deferred makes the heart sick (Proverbs 13 : 12 KJV), but hope revived heals it. As you dare to expect again, joy begins to bubble beneath the surface. God never wastes tears; they water future testimonies.

Faith that believes again rewrites narratives. Sarah laughed in disbelief once, but later laughed in delight. Peter denied, but then declared. God's grace invites you to start over. Believe again for love, for purpose, for miracles. Heaven still responds to faith's whisper.

So, breathe, beloved. Trust again. What you lost cannot compare to what's on the way.

REFLECTIVE STANCE:

What dream or prayer do I need to believe in again?

____

____

____

"Faith doesn't ignore heartbreak; it decides to hope again anyway."
— Rev. Unnia L. Pettus, Ph.D.

PRAYER:

Lord, thank You for restoring my belief. Heal the bruised places in my faith. Help me to trust You beyond my tears and disappointment. Teach me to expect again without fear of failure. Breathe new hope into old prayers. Revive what has been dormant and renew what has been damaged. Thank You that You are faithful even when I struggle to believe. Today I choose to trust again. In Jesus's name, Amen.

MY FAITH NOTES FOR TODAY

____

____

____

MY FAITH DECLARATION:

I will not quit; I will reap because I refuse to faint.

____

____

____

DAY 9
Faith That Stands Still
— Exodus 14:13–14 —
Moses at the Red Sea

"I have fought a good fight, I have finished my course, I have kept the faith."
— 2 Timothy 4:7 (KJV)

DEVOTIONAL

Faith that finishes strong is the faith that refuses to retire from obedience. Paul's final letter is not a lament of fatigue but a declaration of fulfillment. He had endured shipwrecks, beatings, and betrayals, yet he could still say with confidence, "I have kept the faith." Finishing strong means you never stop believing, even when the race changes pace. Anyone can start with zeal; it takes grace to cross the finish line with integrity.

The Christian life is a marathon, not a sprint. Along the way, enthusiasm wanes, friends drift, and unexpected detours appear. But strength is renewed when purpose is remembered. Paul's endurance was anchored in his assignment. When you know why you run, weariness cannot win. Faith keeps its focus not on the applause of men but on the crown of righteousness waiting at the end.

Finishing strong often means finishing scarred. The same hands that heal others may carry their own wounds. Jesus bore nail prints when He declared, "It is finished." Completion, not comfort, marks success. Every scar becomes a signature of survival. Faith doesn't deny pain; it redeems it. If you are limping toward your finish line, remember: grace runs beside you.

Sometimes finishing strong requires letting go of what slows you down. Hebrews 12:1 tells us to "lay aside every weight." Some burdens are not sins—they're simply too heavy for the next season. Faith discerns what to carry and what to cast. Even good things can become hindrances if they hinder growth.

The final stretch is usually the fiercest. Opposition intensifies near breakthrough. That's why faith fixes its eyes on Jesus, not the clock. When you reach the end of yourself, divine strength begins. Paul learned, "When I am weak, then am I strong." God's finishers run on grace, not adrenaline.

Finishing strong also means finishing grateful. Paul gave thanks for companions, for churches, for mercy. Gratitude sustains momentum. Each answered prayer is proof that God has been faithful through every mile. You may not be where you hoped to be, but you are farther than you used to be.

Run your race with joy. Heaven measures success not by speed but by steadfastness. When you finish strong, you declare that the same faith that started you has sustained you.

REFLECTIVE STANCE:
What does finishing strong look like in my current season of life?

____

____

____

"Faith doesn't fade at the finish line—it fuels you to cross it."
— Rev. Unnia L. Pettus, Ph.D.

PRAYER:
Lord, thank You for the strength to keep running. When I grow weary, remind me that Your grace never quits. Help me to finish my course with joy, faith, and focus. Remove every weight that slows me and every doubt that distracts me. Let endurance rise in me until the race You began is complete. When I cross each finish line, may You receive the glory. Thank You that the same hand that started my story will seal it in victory. In Jesus's name, Amen.

MY FAITH NOTES FOR TODAY

MY FAITH DECLARATION:
I will finish strong through the grace that never fails.

DAY 10
Faith That Sees the Sunrise
— Psalm 30:5 —
David

"And Jesus looking upon them saith, With men it is impossible, but not with God: for with God all things are possible."
— Mark 10:27 (KJV)

DEVOTIONAL

Breakthrough faith believes that barriers are invitations for God to show His strength. From Jericho's walls to prison doors in Acts 16, every breakthrough began with a believer who refused to bow to impossibility. Faith does not ignore obstacles—it introduces them to omnipotence. Where human effort ends, divine intervention begins.

Joshua faced walls so thick they mocked reason. Instead of engineering ladders, he obeyed God's strange command to march and shout. The walls fell because obedience became worship. Sometimes breakthrough doesn't come by pushing harder but by praising louder. When you move in faith, heaven moves in power.

Breakthrough often hides behind persistence. The woman with the issue of blood pressed through the crowd until she touched His garment. Her desperation met His divinity, and her body responded to belief. Faith refuses to settle for almost. It pushes past the opinions of others to reach the promise of God.

But breakthrough isn't always outward. Sometimes the greatest walls are internal—fear, unforgiveness, or insecurity. Gideon's breakthrough began when he believed God's word over his own weakness. Your inner agreement determines your outer advancement. As Proverbs 23:7 declares, "As he thinketh in his heart, so is he." When your mind aligns with God's truth, mountains move before your eyes.

Breakthrough faith requires bold speech. The prophet Elisha told King Joash to strike the ground with arrows; his half-hearted effort limited the victory. Faith speaks with full force. Declare healing while you're still hurting, abundance while resources seem absent, peace while storms still rage. Your words create atmospheres where miracles manifest.

Every breakthrough begins as a belief that refuses to quit. Paul and Silas sang until shackles snapped. Their praise unlocked prison doors because it first unlocked heaven's attention. Faith-filled sound carries supernatural strength. Worship is the war cry of winners.

When breakthrough comes, remember it was never your strength but God's sovereignty. Give Him glory and go again—someone else needs the testimony your trial produced. Faith that sees breakthrough keeps believing long after the first victory.

REFLECTIVE STANCE:
Where do I need to believe God for breakthrough today?

____

____

____

"Faith sees walls as opportunities for worship and impossibilities as invitations to witness."
— Rev. Unnia L. Pettus, Ph.D.

PRAYER:
Father, thank You that nothing is impossible with You. Break every barrier that blocks Your will in my life. Teach me to praise before the promise, to obey before I understand, and to trust before I triumph. Let my faith create atmospheres where Your power flows freely. Give me courage to believe again for miracles, signs, and wonders. May every wall fall, every chain break, and every doubt dissolve under Your Word. In Jesus's name, Amen.

MY FAITH NOTES FOR TODAY

____

57

____

____

MY FAITH DECLARATION:

I will believe for breakthrough because my God is unstoppable.

____

____

____

Days 11 ~ 20
Faith That Fights

DAY 11
Faith That Refuses to Bow
— Daniel 3:16–18 —
Shadrach, Meshach & Abednego

"Also I heard the voice of the Lord, saying, Whom shall I send, and who will go for us? Then said I, Here am I; send me."
— Isaiah 6 : 8 (KJV)

DEVOTIONAL

Every believer eventually stands at the crossroads between comfort and calling. Isaiah's response, "Here am I; send me," was not born from convenience but from conviction. Responsive faith doesn't wait for perfect conditions; it responds because obedience outweighs hesitation. The presence of God always provokes purpose. When Isaiah saw the Lord high and lifted up, everything else lost its power to intimidate him.

Faith that answers the call requires surrender. God rarely reveals the full itinerary—He simply says, "Go." Abraham left familiar ground for unseen promise. Moses answered from a burning bush with trembling hands. Mary said, "Be it unto me according to thy word." Each response birthed a new movement of grace. God doesn't need ability; He blesses availability.

Responsive faith listens more than it argues. It trusts that divine direction outweighs human logic. Isaiah's "yes" didn't erase his fear; it eclipsed it. Every assignment begins with agreement. Sometimes God speaks through whispers, sometimes through waiting—but always with purpose. When He calls your name, He already knows your capability because He created your capacity.

Answering the call means accepting change. Obedience always alters your schedule. Jonah ran the wrong way and learned that delayed obedience brings detours. Isaiah teaches us that when God touches your lips with fire, He also transforms your life with favor. You can't meet God and remain the same.

Responsive faith also accepts divine timing. The call may be immediate, but the commissioning is a process. David was anointed long before he was enthroned. Don't despise the preparation; it proves your readiness. God often tests availability before visibility.

Say yes again. Say yes when it's hard. Say yes when it's humbling. Every "Yes, Lord" echoes in eternity. Faith that answers the call doesn't negotiate—it yields. When you surrender, heaven starts aligning things you can't see yet.

REFLECTIVE STANCE:
What is God calling me to say "yes" to right now?

____

____

____

"Faith that responds becomes the bridge between God's voice and God's victory."
— Rev. Unnia L. Pettus, Ph.D.

PRAYER:
Lord, I hear You calling. Remove the fear that makes me hesitate. Touch my heart like You touched Isaiah's lips—purify me and send me. Wherever You lead, I will follow. Teach me that obedience opens doors no opportunity can match. I surrender my plans to Your purpose. Let my life be an answer to Your question, 'Whom shall I send?' Here am I, Lord. Send me. In Jesus's name, Amen.

MY FAITH NOTES FOR TODAY

MY FAITH DECLARATION:
I say "yes" to God's call with a trusting heart.

DAY 12
Faith That Wrestles and Wins
— Genesis 32:26–30 —
Jacob

"By faith Abraham, when he was called to go out into a place which he should after receive for an inheritance, obeyed; and he went out, not knowing whither he went."
— Hebrews 11:8 (KJV)

DEVOTIONAL

Faith often begins where instructions end. Abraham's journey shows that trust sometimes travels without a map. Responsive faith moves when all you have is a promise. God said, "Go," and Abraham went. He didn't know the destination, but he knew the voice. Sometimes that's all you need—certainty in the One who speaks, even when the route is unclear.

Obedience precedes understanding. We often demand details before devotion, but God reveals direction as we move. The GPS of heaven says, "Proceed to the route and I will show you the way."

Each step uncovers the next instruction. Abraham pitched tents because faith travels light. He held possessions loosely, but the promise tightly.

Faith that moves without knowing requires courage to walk away from comfort. Ur was home, secure, familiar. But faith chose forward over familiar. Many miss miracles because they cling to certainty. The first step of obedience is often the hardest but always the holiest.

Moving without knowing is not reckless—it's reliant. Abraham's faith was anchored in God's character, not clarity. He trusted the promise more than the path. When we walk by faith and not by sight (2 Corinthians 5:7), we exchange control for communion. Faith grows best in uncertainty because it forces dependence on God's daily guidance.

There will be moments when God asks you to move while others stay. Don't seek validation from those without your vision. When God told Abraham to look up and count the stars, He was reminding him that the journey of faith always leads to something bigger than you imagined.

The blessing of faith is not found in knowing where you're going, but in knowing Who goes with you. Every mile of uncertainty became an altar of trust. Your steps may not make sense now, but they will lead to something sacred later.

REFLECTIVE STANCE:
Where is God asking me to trust Him without details?

____

____

____

"Faith is the courage to walk into tomorrow holding only God's hand."
— Rev. Unnia L. Pettus, Ph.D.

PRAYER:
Lord, thank You for ordering my steps even when I can't see the path. Give me the courage to move at Your word. Silence the fear that demands details and strengthen my trust in Your timing. Help me to remember that faith is not about knowing everything but knowing You. Guide my footsteps into the future You've prepared.
In Jesus's name, Amen.

MY FAITH NOTES FOR TODAY

____

____

____

MY FAITH DECLARATION:

I will move in faith even when I don't know what's next.

____

____

____

DAY 13
Faith That Shuts the Lions' Mouths
— Daniel 6:22 —
Daniel

"But they that wait upon the Lord shall renew their strength; they shall mount up with wings as eagles; they shall run, and not be weary; and they shall walk, and not faint."
— Isaiah 40 : 31 (KJV)

DEVOTIONAL

Faith that waits is not passive; it is posture. Waiting on God is an active trust that His timing is perfect even when life feels paused. Isaiah wrote to weary believers who had grown impatient, wondering if God had forgotten them. But waiting is never wasted when it's done in worship. Every delay refines dependence.

In Scripture, those who waited well were rewarded. Abraham and Sarah waited twenty-five years for Isaac. Joseph waited thirteen years for his dream. David waited to ascend the throne. Each season of waiting prepared their hearts to carry what they had prayed for. God delays to develop.

Waiting reveals what's in your worship. When the answer seems slow, faith refuses to substitute patience with panic. The word "renew" in Hebrew, chālaph, means to exchange—our weakness for His strength. Waiting, then, becomes an exchange counter for divine energy. Those who wait upon the Lord don't just survive delay—they soar above discouragement.

Faith that waits speaks differently. It doesn't complain; it confesses. Instead of "When, Lord?" it declares "Whenever, Lord." Trust matures when timing is surrendered. Mary and Martha thought Jesus was late for Lazarus, but He was right on time for resurrection.

Sometimes God keeps you waiting because the miracle must meet maturity. If He gave it too soon, you'd mistake the blessing for the blesser. Faith that waits is the evidence of trust in unseen preparation. God is arranging what your eyes can't see yet.

So, rest without retreat. Waiting is worship disguised as stillness. When the wind of the Spirit lifts you, it's not because you forced flight but because you remained faithful on the ground.

REFLECTIVE STANCE:
What lesson is God teaching me in my waiting season?

____

____

____

"Faith doesn't fight the wait; it finds God's strength inside it."
— Rev. Unnia L. Pettus, Ph.D.

PRAYER:
Lord, thank You for reminding me that Your delays are not denials. Teach me to wait with worship and patience. Exchange my weariness for Your strength. When I feel forgotten, whisper that You are still working. Help me soar above discouragement and trust the timing of Your hand. I believe You will fulfill every promise in its perfect season. In Jesus's name, Amen.

MY FAITH NOTES FOR TODAY

____

____

____

MY FAITH DECLARATION:
I will wait on God and find new strength every day.

____

____

____

DAY 14
Faith That Stretches Beyond Comfort
— 1 Kings 17:8–16 —
Widow of Zarephath

"And immediately they left their nets, and followed Him."
— Matthew 4:20 (KJV)

DEVOTIONAL

When Jesus called His first disciples, they didn't schedule obedience—they seized it. Faith that responds immediately refuses to procrastinate the will of God. Peter and Andrew dropped their nets because revelation outweighed hesitation. Immediate obedience opens doors delayed obedience keeps closed.

The difference between a moment and a movement is response time. Throughout Scripture, instant obedience released instant power. When the woman with the issue of blood touched Jesus immediately, virtue flowed immediately. When the centurion said, "Speak the word only," healing happened that same hour. God still honors quick faith.

Faith that acts immediately isn't impulsive—it's inspired. The Spirit quickens you when timing is divine. Delayed responses can dull destiny. Every time God gives an instruction, He also releases the grace to obey it right then. That's why procrastination often feels heavy—it resists divine momentum.

Immediate faith recognizes opportunity hidden in obedience. The fishermen didn't know they'd become apostles; they only knew Who called. Your "yes" today can unlock someone else's salvation tomorrow. Faith that moves immediately says, "I may not have all the answers, but I trust the One giving directions."

Sometimes, immediate action means leaving what's familiar. The disciples left a steady income for an uncertain impact. But they gained purpose that provision could never buy. When you act quickly on God's word, you announce your trust in His supply.

The word "immediately" appears repeatedly in Mark's Gospel because Kingdom work moves at Kingdom pace. Heaven responds to humans who move without hesitation. Faith delayed often becomes faith diminished.

REFLECTIVE STANCE:

Where is God calling me to act immediately in obedience?

____

____

____

"Delayed obedience is disguised disobedience;

faith moves when

God speaks.

— Rev. Unnia L. Pettus, Ph.D.

PRAYER:

Father, forgive me for the times I've hesitated when You called. Today, I choose to obey immediately. Strengthen my resolve to move in step with Your Spirit. Make me sensitive to divine timing and bold in response. Let my quick obedience become a testimony of trust. May my actions align with heaven's agenda. In Jesus's name, Amen.

MY FAITH NOTES FOR TODAY

____

____

____

MY FAITH DECLARATION:

I will respond quickly when God calls; my faith moves now.

____

____

____

DAY 15
Faith That Walks on Water
— Matthew 14:28–31 —
Peter

"For God hath not given us the spirit of fear; but of power, and of love, and of a sound mind."
— 2 Timothy 1:7 (KJV)

DEVOTIONAL

Fear is the enemy's favorite weapon because it paralyzes potential. Timothy's timid heart needed Paul's reminder that fear is not a divine deposit. Faith responds to fear by remembering the source of courage—God Himself. The Spirit within us is not scared; He is strong.

Faith that overcomes fear replaces panic with purpose. When Goliath mocked Israel, Saul froze, but David ran toward the battle with belief. The difference wasn't size—it was sight. Faith sees possibility where fear sees paralysis. Every fearful moment is an opportunity to prove who controls your focus.

Fear whispers "what if." Faith shouts "even if." The three Hebrew boys didn't deny the furnace—they defied it. They said, "Our God is able," but even if He doesn't, we still won't bow. That's responsive faith—bold trust that obedience is worth the outcome.

Overcoming fear doesn't mean you never feel it; it means fear no longer decides for you. Peter stepped onto the water trembling, but he still stepped. Courage is movement despite emotion. The Greek word for sound mind, sōphroneō, means disciplined thinking. Faith trains your thoughts to focus on truth, not threat.

You overcome fear through declaration. Speak Scripture until confidence rises. Remind fear that it's evicted. The cross proved that perfect love casts out fear (1 John 4 : 18). The same love that rescued you keeps you steady.

When fear knocks, let faith answer the door. Every victory over fear strengthens spiritual muscle for the next battle. Eventually, fear will realize it's wasting time attacking a believer who knows their authority.

REFLECTIVE STANCE:
What fear is God asking me to confront with faith?

____

____

____

"Faith doesn't deny fear—it dethrones it."
— Rev. Unnia L. Pettus, Ph.D.

PRAYER:

Lord, thank You for giving me power, love, and a sound mind. Silence the voices of fear that try to drown out Your truth. Fill my heart with courage rooted in Your promises. Remind me that perfect love drives out all fear. Today, I step forward in faith, trusting that You are greater than what scares me. In Jesus's name, Amen.

MY FAITH NOTES FOR TODAY

MY FAITH DECLARATION:

Fear has no hold on me; faith fuels my focus.

DAY 16 Faith That Refuses to Quit
— Luke 18:1–8 —
Persistent Widow

"My son, attend to my words; incline thine ear unto my sayings."
— Proverbs 4 : 20 (KJV)

DEVOTIONAL

Faith that listens grows faster than faith that lectures. Many believers talk to God but never pause to hear Him speak. Solomon reminds us that spiritual success begins with attentiveness. The Hebrew word for "incline" means to stretch or bend toward — to lean in. Faith that listens leans into God's voice even when it whispers.

Throughout Scripture, listening preceded miracles. Noah listened before building. Moses listened before leading. Mary listened before birthing the Savior. Jesus Himself said, "My sheep hear my voice." (John 10:27, NIV) Hearing God is the hinge upon which destiny turns.

Faith that listens requires quiet surrender. The world is loud; fear and doubt are noisy neighbors. But divine direction often arrives in stillness. Elijah didn't find God in the earthquake or the fire, but in a still small voice. That voice still speaks when we silence the chaos.

When you listen, God gives strategy. Joshua conquered Jericho because he followed precise instructions: march, stay silent, then shout. One missed command could have cost the miracle. Many prayers fail not because God didn't speak, but because we didn't wait to listen.

Listening faith produces lasting fruit. It transforms impulse into insight. Every obedient ear receives supernatural clarity. Listening builds intimacy because it's impossible to mishear someone you spend time with daily.

So, before acting, pause. Before deciding, pray. Before rushing, rest. God's timing is always tied to His voice. If you want divine results, start with divine instructions.

REFLECTIVE STANCE:
How can I become more intentional about hearing God daily?

____

____

____

"Faith flourishes when the heart listens longer than the mouth speaks."
— Rev. Unnia L. Pettus, Ph.D.

PRAYER:

Lord, teach me to listen. Quiet the noise of worry and hurry. Tune my ear to Your Spirit's frequency. When You speak, let my heart obey immediately. Give me discernment to recognize Your whisper amid distraction. I long to follow Your instructions and walk in wisdom. Speak, Lord—Your servant is listening. In Jesus's name, Amen.

MY FAITH NOTES FOR TODAY

____

____

____

MY FAITH DECLARATION:

I will lean in and listen to God's voice every day.

____

____

____

DAY 17
Faith That Breaks Barriers
— Mark 2:1–12 —
The Paralytic and His Friends

*"And whatsoever ye do, do it heartily, as to the Lord,
and not unto men."*
— Colossians 3 : 23 (KJV)

DEVOTIONAL

Responsive faith doesn't wait for recognition—it works for the reward that only heaven gives. True faith serves in secret, trusting God to bring visibility in His time. Jesus washed feet before He wore a crown, proving that humility is the language of heaven.

Service tests the sincerity of faith. The disciples argued about greatness, but Jesus redefined it: "The greatest among you will be your servant." (Matthew 23 : 11, NIV) When faith fuels service, your heart finds joy in obedience, not applause.

Faith that serves without spotlight means cleaning the unseen, helping the unthanked, and loving the undeserving. Ruth gleaned in obscurity before being noticed by Boaz. God often watches how we handle the hidden before He promotes us to the public.

Serving strengthens faith because it keeps pride powerless. When you serve others, you mirror the Master. Every act of kindness becomes a sermon without words. Even when unnoticed, heaven records it.

Faith-filled service also breaks selfishness. It reminds you that life is not about status but stewardship. God trusts servants with secrets. Elisha poured water for Elijah before receiving a double portion.

So, keep showing up even when nobody claps. God sees, God rewards, and God remembers. The spotlight may miss you, but grace never will.

REFLECTIVE STANCE:
Where can I serve quietly while trusting God to see me?

____

____

____

"When you serve in silence, heaven makes the announcement."
— Rev. Unnia L. Pettus, Ph.D.

PRAYER:
Lord, thank You for teaching me to serve from the heart, not for headlines. Purify my motives and increase my humility. Help me to see service as sacred. Whether washing feet or carrying burdens, let my actions reflect Your love. Use my life to make others see You. In Jesus's name, Amen.

MY FAITH NOTES FOR TODAY

____

____

____

MY FAITH DECLARATION:
I will serve faithfully even when no one is watching.

____

____

____

DAY 18
Faith That Speaks Life
— Proverbs 18:21 —
Ezekiel and the Dry Bones

"Death and life are in the power of the tongue: and they that love it
shall eat the fruit thereof."
— Proverbs 18 : 21 (KJV)

DEVOTIONAL

Faith speaks what it seeks, not what it sees. God formed the world with words, and as His children, we create atmospheres through confession. What you speak consistently becomes what you see eventually. Responsive faith learns to align language with life.

The woman with the issue of blood said within herself, "If I may but touch His garment, I shall be whole." Her miracle began in her mouth. She didn't wait to feel better; she spoke better. Your confession is the seed of your transformation.

Faith that speaks life refuses to echo negativity. When Ezekiel stood in a valley of dry bones, God asked, "Can these bones live?" Ezekiel answered, "Lord, Thou knowest." Then God said, "Prophesy." Sometimes life changes only when you start declaring what God says instead of describing what you see.

Words build worlds. Speak healing in the hospital, peace in the storm, provision in lack. Job declared, "Though He slay me, yet will I trust Him." (Job 13 : 15) That's faith refusing to let pain silence praise.

Speaking life doesn't ignore reality; it invokes divinity. Every promise God made still responds to faith-filled words. When you decree, heaven agrees.

So, open your mouth and partner with God's plan. Silence is permission for stagnation. Let your words match your worship.

REFLECTIVE STANCE:
What life-giving words do I need to start speaking today?

____

____

____

"What you say today shapes what you stand on tomorrow."
— Rev. Unnia L. Pettus, Ph.D.

PRAYER:
Father, help me guard my tongue and guide my talk. Let every word I speak agree with Your Word. Cancel every negative confession I've ever spoken. Teach me to prophesy life over dead situations. Fill my mouth with gratitude and my heart with faith. May my speech draw others to You. In Jesus's name, Amen.

MY FAITH NOTES FOR TODAY

____

____

____

MY FAITH DECLARATION:
I speak life, hope, and faith in every situation.

____

____

____

DAY 19
Faith That Rises From the Ashes
— Job 42:10 —
Job

"I will bless thee, and make thy name great; and thou shalt be a blessing."
— Genesis 12 : 2 (KJV)

DEVOTIONAL

Faith that blesses others reflects the heart of Abraham, who was chosen not just to be blessed but to be a blessing. God's abundance is never meant to end with you—it's designed to flow through you. When faith matures, generosity multiplies.

Blessing others is both calling and covenant. Every seed sown into another's life becomes proof of partnership with heaven. Jesus went about doing good because goodness is the fruit of godly faith.

When we bless others, we imitate God's generosity. The widow of Zarephath gave her last meal to Elijah and discovered that her supply was tied to her sharing. Giving always grows what gratitude guards.

Faith that blesses others doesn't wait for excess; it starts with empathy. Peter said, "Silver and gold have

I none; but such as I have give I thee." (Acts 3 : 6) You always have something—a prayer, a smile, a word of encouragement.

Blessing others unlocks hidden favor. Abraham's obedience birthed nations. Job prayed for his friends and God restored him double. When you focus on being a conduit, God ensures you never run dry.

Let your faith leave fingerprints on the lives you touch. Blessing others proves your faith is alive and active.

REFLECTIVE STANCE:
How can I intentionally bless someone this week?

____

____

____

"The blessed life is the life that keeps blessing."
— Rev. Unnia L. Pettus, Ph.D.

PRAYER:
*Lord, thank You for every blessing You've given me.
Show me who needs what I carry. Make me generous
with time, love, and resources. Let my faith overflow
into kindness. Use me to lift burdens and brighten
hearts. May my hands reflect Your heart.
In Jesus's name, Amen.*

MY FAITH NOTES FOR TODAY

____

____

____

MY FAITH DECLARATION:
I am blessed to be a blessing every day.

____

____

____

DAY 20
Faith That Brings the Walls Down
— Joshua 6:20 —
Joshua and Jericho

"Rejoice with them that do rejoice."
— Romans 12 : 15 (KJV)

DEVOTIONAL

Responsive faith doesn't compete; it celebrates. Real faith is secure enough to shout for someone else's success. Jealousy says, "Why not me?" Faith says, "Praise God for them!" When you rejoice with others, you prove that you trust God's timing for you.

David danced when the Ark returned because celebration restores joy to community. Saul, however, grew bitter when others praised David. The difference was perspective. Comparison kills contentment, but faith keeps you focused on your own lane.

Celebrating others enlarges your capacity. If you can shout for their harvest, God can trust you with your own. When Elizabeth heard Mary's greeting, her baby leaped—proof that joy is contagious when shared.

Faith that celebrates others believes the same God who blessed them hasn't run out of miracles. Envy limits expectancy. When you clap for another, you create atmosphere for your own breakthrough.

Celebrate loudly. Encourage publicly. Honor sincerely. When we build each other up, the whole Body of Christ rises higher.

Your time is coming, but meanwhile, dance for your neighbor. The blessing next door is evidence that God is in the neighborhood!

REFLECTIVE STANCE:
Whose victory can I celebrate this week?

____

____

____

"Faith doesn't compete with others—it completes what God began in you."
— Rev. Unnia L. Pettus, Ph.D.

PRAYER:
Father, thank You for teaching me to rejoice with others. Deliver me from comparison and fill me with compassion. Let gratitude overflow when others win. Keep my heart free of envy and full of encouragement. I celebrate what You're doing everywhere because I know You're not finished with me.
In Jesus's name, Amen.

MY FAITH NOTES FOR TODAY

____

____

____

My Faith Declaration:
I celebrate others' victories and trust God for mine.

____

____

____

Days 21 ~ 30
Faith That
Overcomes

DAY 21
Faith That Moves Forward
— Philippians 3:13–14 —
Paul

"Men ought always to pray, and not to faint."
— Luke 18:1 (KJV)

DEVOTIONAL

Persistent faith refuses to hang up on heaven. Jesus told the parable of the persistent widow to remind us that prayer is not persuasion—it's participation. The widow didn't stop coming until the unjust judge responded. If a corrupt man could yield to persistence, how much more will a righteous Father answer His children?

Faith that keeps praying through doesn't focus on delay but on devotion. It says, "Even if I haven't seen it yet, I'll keep seeking." Elijah prayed for rain seven times before a small cloud appeared. Daniel prayed twenty-one days before the angel broke through. Each prayer moved heaven closer to earth.

Persistence is proof of trust. The Greek word proseuchomai means to continue asking earnestly. Prayer stretches faith like spiritual exercise. Every "Amen" strengthens spiritual muscle. God often uses delay to refine desire. If you stop praying too soon, you might forfeit what was already forming.

Persistent faith also prays with expectation. The widow didn't show up to complain; she came to collect. Expectancy is evidence of belief. When we pray believing that God hears, we align ourselves with His power. James 5 : 16 reminds us, "The effectual fervent prayer of a righteous man availeth much."

Sometimes prayer feels repetitive—but repetition is revelation. It reveals who really reigns. Persistent prayer changes you before it changes things. By the time the answer arrives, you've been transformed by the waiting.

So, pray again. Cry again. Believe again. Every tear is a testimony waiting for timing. The same God who heard Hannah, Elijah, and Daniel still hears you.

REFLECTIVE STANCE:

What prayer have I almost stopped praying that God wants me to continue?

____

____

____

"Persistence in prayer isn't pestering God—

it's proving you trust

His promise."

— Rev. Unnia L. Pettus, Ph.D.

PRAYER:

Lord, thank You for reminding me that prayer still works even when progress feels slow. Strengthen my faith to keep praying through pain and delay. Let my persistence please You. Teach me to pray from confidence, not desperation. I trust that Your silence is not absence but strategy. I believe the answer is on the way.
In Jesus's name, Amen.

MY FAITH NOTES FOR TODAY

____

____

____

MY FAITH DECLARATION:

I will keep praying until heaven answers.

____

____

____

DAY 22
Faith That Waits in the Wilderness
— Exodus 16:35 —
Israel in the Desert

"For a just man falleth seven times, and riseth up again."
— Proverbs 24 : 16 (KJV)

DEVOTIONAL

Faith that lasts learns how to get up. Setbacks don't disqualify you; they develop you. The righteous may fall, but grace always gives another rise. Peter denied Jesus three times, but Jesus still called him "rock." Resurrection power revives those who refuse to stay down.

Setbacks expose the strength of your stance. Anyone can shout on mountaintops, but true faith still worships in valleys. Job lost everything yet declared, "Though He slay me, yet will I trust Him." (Job 13 : 15 KJV) That's faith refusing to flinch.

When you fall, don't focus on failure; focus on forward. God uses failure as fertilizer for future fruit. Joseph's betrayal became his bridge to the palace.

Paul's imprisonment birthed letters that still free souls today.

Standing again requires remembering who holds you. Ephesians 6 : 13 says, "Having done all, to stand." Standing is warfare. It declares to the enemy, "You knocked me down, but not out." Every comeback glorifies Christ.

Faith after setbacks is stronger because it's scarred. Scars are proof that pain didn't prevail. They remind you that what hurt you didn't halt you.

So rise again—pray again—believe again. Heaven celebrates every soul who stands where hell expected surrender.

REFLECTIVE STANCE:

How can I rise from my latest setback with greater faith?

____

____

____

"Setbacks aren't signs of defeat; they're setups for resurrection."

— Rev. Unnia L. Pettus, Ph.D.

PRAYER:
Lord, thank You for lifting me when life knocks me down. Remind me that Your grace is greater than my mistakes. Turn every setback into a stage for Your strength. Renew my courage to stand firm in faith. Let my testimony encourage others to rise. In Jesus's name, Amen.

MY FAITH NOTES FOR TODAY

MY FAITH DECLARATION:
I will rise again through the strength of Christ.

DAY 23
Faith That Finds Favor
— Esther 4:14 —
Esther

"Be not weary in well doing: for in due season we shall reap, if we faint not."
— Galatians 6 : 9 (KJV)

DEVOTIONAL

Faith gets tired too. Paul's encouragement reminds us that fatigue doesn't mean failure. Weariness whispers, "Quit," but faith whispers back, "Wait." Those who persevere through exhaustion find supernatural energy on the other side.

Elijah, the mighty prophet, once sat under a juniper tree saying, "It is enough." God didn't rebuke him; He replenished him. The angel brought bread and water, then told him, "The journey is too great for thee." Even great faith needs divine refreshment.

Persistent faith rests strategically. It knows that rhythm sustains revival. Jesus often withdrew to pray, not to escape people but to stay powered by purpose. If the Savior needed solitude, so do we.

Fatigue often disguises spiritual warfare. The enemy can't steal your calling, so he tries to drain your energy. That's why God invites you to cast burdens and receive rest.

Faith that fights fatigue doesn't run on feelings—it runs on fire. Jeremiah said, "His word was in my heart as a burning fire shut up in my bones." (Jeremiah 20 : 9 KJV) When you feel empty, let His Word refill your flame.

Keep sowing, keep serving, keep believing. The harvest is hidden in "due season," not your season. Every weary prayer still waters the promise.

REFLECTIVE STANCE:

What do I need to lay down so God can renew my strength?

____

____

____

"Faith doesn't ignore exhaustion—it invites God to refuel it."

— Rev. Unnia L. Pettus, Ph.D.

PRAYER:

Lord, renew me when I am weary. Restore joy where fatigue has settled. Feed my soul with Your presence until my strength returns. Help me not to faint before the harvest. Teach me that resting is part of trusting. Thank You for being my strength when I am weak. In Jesus's name, Amen.

MY FAITH NOTES FOR TODAY

____

____

____

MY FAITH DECLARATION:
I will not faint; I will reap because I refuse to quit.

____

____

____

DAY 24
Faith That Believes Again
— John 11:25–27 —
Martha at Lazarus' Tomb

"We are troubled on every side, yet not distressed; we are perplexed, but not in despair."
— 2 Corinthians 4 : 8 (KJV)

DEVOTIONAL

Pressure exposes what's real. Paul's words describe the paradox of persistent faith—crushed but not cursed, pressed but not perishing. Believers are not exempt from struggle; they're empowered to endure it.

Faith under pressure discovers peace in paradox. The Greek word for "troubled" means "crowded." Pressure compresses, but it also clarifies. It pushes out distractions so only devotion remains.

Jesus prayed under the pressure of Gethsemane until sweat became blood. Persistence held Him there—love kept Him going. If the Son of God endured pressure, so can we by His power.

Faith that endures pressure sees purpose in pain. Diamonds form under it. Oil flows from olives only after crushing. What feels like breaking is actually birthing.

Pressure cannot silence praise. Paul and Silas sang in prison, and the earth shook. Their chains fell, not because the door opened, but because faith did.

The devil applies pressure to stop prayer; God allows it to prove power. Your persistence is proof you still believe. Keep pressing until breakthrough replaces burden.

REFLECTIVE STANCE:
How can I glorify God while I'm still under pressure?

____

____

____

"Pressure doesn't destroy faith—it distills it."
— Rev. Unnia L. Pettus, Ph.D.

PRAYER:
Lord, thank You for being my anchor when life presses hard. Give me grace to stay steadfast. Let pressure purify, not paralyze. Remind me that oil only flows after crushing. Fill me with endurance to keep believing. Turn my burden into breakthrough.
In Jesus's name, Amen.

MY FAITH NOTES FOR TODAY

MY FAITH DECLARATION:
I am pressed but not broken—my faith still stands.

DAY 25
Faith That Stands in the Gap
— Ezekiel 22:30 —
Intercessors and Prophets

"My brethren, count it all joy when ye fall into divers temptations."
— James 1 : 2 (KJV)

DEVOTIONAL

Pain often preaches the loudest sermons. James tells believers to count trials as joy—not because they feel good, but because they produce good. Faith that perseveres sees purpose through pain.

Joseph's journey from pit to palace proves that painful seasons hide divine strategy. Betrayal, bondage, and blame couldn't block his blessing. He later told his brothers, "Ye thought evil against me; but God meant it unto good." (Genesis 50 : 20 KJV)

Pain purifies motives and solidifies trust. When Job sat in ashes, he refused to curse God. Instead, he said, "I know my Redeemer liveth." Pain matured his faith from conditional to confident.

Persistent faith doesn't pretend pain doesn't hurt—it declares that hurt won't have the last word. Tears are not signs of weakness but seeds of worship.

Psalm 126 : 5 promises, "They that sow in tears shall reap in joy."

Faith perseveres by focusing on promise, not predicament. Jesus endured the cross "for the joy set before Him." (Hebrews 12 : 2 NIV) He looked beyond suffering to salvation.

Your current pain is preparing future purpose. Endure, expect, and emerge. After every cross, resurrection follows.

REFLECTIVE STANCE:

What purpose might God be revealing through my current pain?

____

____

____

"Faith doesn't deny pain — it declares purpose in spite of it."

— Rev. Unnia L. Pettus, Ph.D.

PRAYER:

Father, thank You for walking with me through painful places. Teach me to find joy in the journey. Use my suffering to strengthen my spirit. Let my testimony help others heal. Remind me that pain is temporary but purpose is eternal. I trust that You are working all things together for good.
In Jesus's name, Amen.

MY FAITH NOTES FOR TODAY

____

____

____

MY FAITH DECLARATION:
My pain will produce purpose by God's power.

____

____

____

DAY 26
Faith That Hears in Silence
— 1 Kings 19:11–12 —
Elijah

"Let us hold fast the profession of our faith without wavering; (for He is faithful that promised)."
— Hebrews 10 : 23 (KJV)

DEVOTIONAL

Hope is the heartbeat of faith. When circumstances shake, hope steadies the soul. The writer of Hebrews reminds us to hold fast—cling, grip, refuse to let go—because the One who promised is still faithful. Persistent faith holds hope when hands grow tired, because it remembers who holds tomorrow.

Abraham held to hope when his body said "impossible." Romans 4 : 18 declares, "Who against hope believed in hope." Hope anchored him when evidence disappeared. Faith feeds on memory: if God did it before, He can do it again.

Hope doesn't ignore reality; it re-interprets it through revelation. When Paul wrote from prison, he still said, "Rejoice in the Lord always." Hope finds praise even behind bars. Persistent believers keep expecting even when experience contradicts expectation.

To hold on to hope, saturate your spirit with Scripture. Every verse is a rope of promise. When storms rage, tie yourself to what God has spoken. David declared, "I had fainted, unless I had believed to see the goodness of the Lord." (Psalm 27 : 13) Hope kept him breathing between battles.

Sometimes hope feels heavy, but it's holy weight training. Each day you refuse despair, your endurance expands. You may bend under burden, but faith makes you bounce back.

Hold on. Help is on the way. The God who began your story hasn't run out of chapters.

REFLECTIVE STANCE:
Where do I need to tighten my grip on hope today?

____

____

____

"Hope is faith's handrail when the climb gets steep."
— Rev. Unnia L. Pettus, Ph.D.

PRAYER:

*Lord, thank You for being faithful when life feels fragile.
Strengthen my grip on hope. Remind me that Your
promises never expire. Teach me to rehearse Your
faithfulness until fear fades. Renew my joy while I wait.
I believe You will finish what You started.
In Jesus's name, Amen.*

MY FAITH NOTES FOR TODAY

____

____

____

MY FAITH DECLARATION:

I will hold on to hope because God is holding me.

____

____

____

DAY 27
Faith That Rebuilds the Temple
— Ezra 3:10–13 —
Zerubbabel

"Be still, and know that I am God."
— Psalm 46 : 10 (KJV)

DEVOTIONAL

The hardest test of faith is not waiting—it's waiting while God seems silent. Silence can sound like absence, but it's often evidence of intimacy. God speaks through stillness to strengthen trust. Persistent faith keeps believing even when heaven is quiet.

Job heard nothing for months, yet never stopped revering God. In his silence, God was scripting restoration. Between Malachi and Matthew, Israel endured four hundred years without a prophet's voice, but the silence birthed the Savior.

Faith that endures silence chooses worship over worry. When you can't hear God, revisit what He already said. The last instruction still carries weight. Silence is not punishment—it's preparation for revelation.

During Jesus' trial, He spoke not a word. Silence can be strength, not weakness. Heaven doesn't need to shout to stay sovereign.

In your quiet seasons, lean into prayer, praise, and patience. God is still present even when He's not audible. The teacher is silent during the test but never leaves the room.

When the sound returns, you'll realize the silence grew your spiritual hearing.

REFLECTIVE STANCE:
What can I learn about God in His silence?

____

____

____

"Silence from God isn't absence—it's an invitation to deeper trust."
— Rev. Unnia L. Pettus, Ph.D.

PRAYER:
Lord, thank You for being near even when You seem quiet. Teach me to be still and trust Your unseen work. Strengthen my heart in the hush. Let peace replace panic and faith rise above frustration. I believe You're speaking through the stillness.
In Jesus's name, Amen.

MY FAITH NOTES FOR TODAY

____

____

____

MY FAITH DECLARATION:
Even in silence, I know God is working for me.

____

____

____

DAY 28
Faith That Survives the Storm
— Mark 4:39 —
Jesus Calms the Sea

"I press toward the mark for the prize of the high calling of God in Christ Jesus."
— Philippians 3:14 (KJV)

DEVOTIONAL

Purpose gives faith direction. Paul wrote these words from prison, proving that confinement can't cancel calling. Persistent faith presses even when progress pauses.

Purpose-driven believers refuse to drift. When opposition rises, purpose reminds them why they started. Nehemiah faced mockers while rebuilding Jerusalem's walls, but said, "I am doing a great work, so that I cannot come down." (Nehemiah 6 : 3 KJV) Faith stays focused when critics shout.

Purpose produces perseverance. You can endure pain when you know it's producing destiny. Jesus, focused on His mission, ignored the crowd's scorn because He saw the joy beyond the cross.

To persist in purpose, keep aligning goals with grace. Ask, "Does this move me closer to God's assignment?" Purpose keeps you pressing in prayer, even when applause fades.

Faith-filled persistence isn't stubbornness—it's spiritual stamina. It remembers that the prize is not position but presence.

Every press proves you're still alive in purpose. The enemy fights hardest when you're closest to fulfillment. Keep pressing; heaven is applauding.

REFLECTIVE STANCE:
Where do I need to press again toward purpose?

____

____

____

"Purpose gives pain a reason and faith a runway."
— Rev. Unnia L. Pettus, Ph.D.

PRAYER:
Lord, thank You for calling me to a purpose larger than my problems. Give me strength to press forward when progress feels slow. Guard my focus from distraction. Let perseverance finish its work in me. I press toward the prize with joy and determination. In Jesus's name, Amen.

MY FAITH NOTES FOR TODAY

____

____

____

MY FAITH DECLARATION:

I will press on with purpose until God's plan prevails.

____

____

____

DAY 29
Faith That Looks Again
— 2 Kings 6:17 —
Elisha and His Servant

"Thy word is a lamp unto my feet, and a light unto my path."
— Psalm 119:105 (KJV)

DEVOTIONAL

Faith walks best when guided by light. God's Word is not a spotlight showing the whole road; it's a lamp revealing the next step. Persistent faith keeps walking even when visibility is low because Scripture lights each moment.

When Israel followed the pillar of fire, they moved when it moved. The Word functions the same—it guides motion, not stagnation. The more you walk in it, the brighter it gets.

Faith anchored in the Word cannot drift. Jesus defeated temptation by saying, "It is written." The Word is a weapon and a compass. It secures footing when emotions wobble.

Daily reading renews direction. The lamp doesn't dim; hearts do. Reignite passion by returning to the pages of promise.

Walking by the Word transforms wanderers into witnesses. Every obedient step testifies that truth still works.

Keep walking. Even if all you see is enough light for today, that's enough for destiny.

REFLECTIVE STANCE:
How can I rely more on Scripture for daily direction?

____

____

____

"Faith walks farther when every step echoes Scripture."

— Rev. Unnia L. Pettus, Ph.D.

PRAYER:
Lord, illuminate my path with Your Word. Let Scripture shape every decision. When darkness surrounds, remind me that Your truth still shines. Keep me walking faithfully, step by step.
In Jesus's name, Amen.

MY FAITH NOTES FOR TODAY

____

____

____

MY FAITH DECLARATION:
I walk by the Word and not by worldly wisdom.

____

____

____

DAY 30
Faith That Conquers Giants
— 1 Samuel 17:45–47 —
David and Goliath

"I will not let Thee go, except Thou bless me."
— Genesis 32:26 (KJV)

DEVOTIONAL

Jacob's midnight wrestle defines persistence. He held on until heaven moved. Faith that never lets go refuses to release God in frustration or fatigue. It clings until blessing breaks forth.

Jacob's grip was desperate yet determined. Wrestling faith happens in prayer rooms and hospital rooms, between fear and faith. It's the cry of every believer who says, "God, I won't stop until You show up."

Persistence provokes transformation. Jacob entered that night as a deceiver and left as Israel, a prince with God. Your wrestle refines identity.

When you cling to God through pain, you prove you value presence over convenience. Many let go too soon, missing the miracle attached to midnight.

Faith that won't let go lives on divine tenacity. It says, "Even if I limp, I'll leave blessed." Every struggle you survive strengthens your spiritual grip.

Hold on until grace changes your name, your walk, your world.

REFLECTIVE STANCE:
What area of my life is God calling me to hold on in faith?

____

____

____

"Breakthrough belongs to believers who refuse to let go."
— Rev. Unnia L. Pettus, Ph.D.

PRAYER:
Lord, I won't let go until You bless me. Strengthen my grip through grief, waiting, and wrestling. Change my name where I've carried shame. Bless my persistence with peace. I trust that every struggle ends in Your strength.
In Jesus's name, Amen.

MY FAITH NOTES FOR TODAY

____

____

____

MY FAITH DECLARATION:
I will cling to God until He completes His promise.

____

____

____

Days 31 ~ 40

Faith That Overflows

DAY 31
Faith That Finds Freedom
— Exodus 12:31–32 —
Moses

"To every thing there is a season, and a time to every purpose under the heaven."
— Ecclesiastes 3:1 (KJV)

DEVOTIONAL

Perfect faith accepts that divine timing never rushes and never fails. We live in a culture that wants everything now—instant messages, instant coffee, instant miracles. But God works in seasons, not seconds. Faith matures when we realize delay is not denial; it is divine development.

Joseph's dreams were delayed for more than a decade. He moved from pit to prison before palace. Each pause shaped him into a man who could handle authority without arrogance. The waiting room of God is the training ground of wisdom.

Perfect faith stops measuring God's love by how quickly He answers. It rests in the truth that the same God who made the promise will make the timing perfect. "He hath made every thing beautiful in his time." (Ecclesiastes 3 : 11 KJV) The beauty of promise blooms only when planted in patience.

When timing tests you, remember Jesus waited thirty years before His public ministry. Even miracles have moments attached to them. The wedding wine ran out before Jesus turned water into something better. He may not come when you call, but He never misses the appointed hour.

Faith that trusts timing also trusts pruning. God delays to prepare. What feels like waiting is often God aligning circumstances, people, and provision. If He gave it too early, it might destroy you instead of developing you.

So, breathe. Let peace do what panic cannot. The clock in heaven keeps perfect time. God is never late—He's simply setting the stage.

REFLECTIVE STANCE:
Where am I struggling to trust God's timing?

____

____

____

"Perfect faith stops checking the clock and starts trusting the Creator."
— Rev. Unnia L. Pettus, Ph.D.

PRAYER:

Lord, thank You for reminding me that Your delays are divine. Teach me to trust Your seasons. Calm my anxious heart when answers take longer than expected. Let patience have her perfect work in me. I believe that everything You promised will arrive right on time. In Jesus's name, Amen.

MY FAITH NOTES FOR TODAY

____

____

____

MY FAITH DECLARATION:

I trust God's timing more than my own timeline.

____

____

____

DAY 32
Faith That Forgives
— Genesis 45:4–8 —
Joseph

*"For I know the plans I have for you, saith the Lord,
plans to prosper you and not to harm you, plans to give
you a future and a hope."*
— Jeremiah 29:11 (NIV)

DEVOTIONAL

Faith becomes perfect when it learns to rest. Rest doesn't mean inactivity; it means inner peace that refuses panic. The exiles of Judah heard Jeremiah's prophecy while living far from home. Yet God said, "I still have plans." Even in foreign places, divine purpose remains.

Resting in God's plan means trusting that the story isn't finished. Joseph rested in prison, David rested in caves, Paul rested in chains—all because they believed purpose could not be postponed. Faith that rests realizes God's blueprint includes both blessings and battles.

When we rest, we release control. Jesus slept through a storm because His trust was greater than His terror. The disciples panicked while Peace personified was in the boat! Perfect faith learns to sleep even when the wind is loud.

To rest is to remember that God writes straight with crooked lines. What feels like detour is often direction. Romans 8:28 reminds us that "all things work together for good." All means all—success and struggle, comfort and correction.

When you can't trace His hand, rest in His heart. He's too wise to be mistaken, too loving to be cruel. Every closed door and every hard season is included in His plan for your growth.

So, exhale. Stop fighting the plan and start flowing in peace. The Author and Finisher of your faith has never lost a manuscript.

REFLECTIVE STANCE:

What area of my life do I need to release to God's plan?

"Rest is the rhythm of faith that knows God never wastes a moment."
— Rev. Unnia L. Pettus, Ph.D.

PRAYER:
*Father, thank You for knowing the plans I cannot see.
Forgive me for the times I fought Your will. Help me to
rest instead of wrestle. Let peace rule my thoughts and
patience guide my pace. I trust that Your plan will
prosper me.
In Jesus's name, Amen.*

MY FAITH NOTES FOR TODAY

____

____

____

MY FAITH DECLARATION:

I rest in God's plan because He is faithful to perform
it.

____

____

____

DAY 33
Faith That Sings in the Dark
— Acts 16:25–26 —
Paul and Silas

"Let this mind be in you, which was also in Christ Jesus."
— Philippians 2:5 (KJV)

DEVOTIONAL

Perfect faith doesn't just believe in Christ—it behaves like Christ. The mind of Christ is humility, compassion, obedience, and love. When faith matures, it mirrors the Master.

Jesus could calm storms because He carried peace within. He could forgive enemies because He was free from ego. Perfect faith asks, "What would Jesus do—and how can I do it with His heart?"

Faith that reflects Christ refuses retaliation and chooses restoration. On the cross, He prayed, "Father, forgive them." That's faith strong enough to love while bleeding. When your character reflects His, you shine where others curse the darkness.

The process of reflection takes polishing. Trials rub away pride and self-reliance until His image appears. 2 Corinthians 3:18 says we are being "transformed into His image from glory to glory." Every hardship is a mirror-making moment.

To reflect Christ means to carry compassion into chaos. Love the difficult. Serve the undeserving. Forgive the unforgivable. That's not weakness—it's Christlikeness.

Your reflection may not be perfect yet, but it's progressing. Each day you surrender, the mirror clears a little more.

REFLECTIVE STANCE:
How can my actions better reflect Christ's heart?

"Faith matures when your reflection starts to resemble your Redeemer."
— Rev. Unnia L. Pettus, Ph.D.

PRAYER:
Lord Jesus, shape my heart to mirror Yours. Remove pride and replace it with patience. Teach me to forgive quickly and love deeply. Let humility be my hallmark. Transform my reactions until they reveal Your righteousness. Make my life a living reflection of Your grace.
In Jesus's name, Amen.

MY FAITH NOTES FOR TODAY

____

____

____

MY FAITH DECLARATION:
I choose to reflect Christ's character in all I do.

____

____

____

DAY 34
Faith That Sees the Promise
— Numbers 13:30 —
Caleb and Joshua

"And be ye kind one to another, tenderhearted, forgiving one another, even as God for Christ's sake hath forgiven you."
— Ephesians 4 : 32 (KJV)

DEVOTIONAL

Perfect faith isn't proven by how high you shout but by how quickly you forgive. Forgiveness is the highest form of faith because it releases what pride wants to hold. Paul urged the church at Ephesus to mirror the mercy they had received. When you forgive, you stop playing judge and start acting like Jesus.

Forgiveness doesn't excuse behavior—it exchanges bondage for blessing. Joseph forgave his brothers who sold him into slavery because he saw God's sovereignty beyond their sin. Perfect faith looks at betrayal and says, "What you meant for evil, God used for good." That kind of mercy requires maturity.

Unforgiveness poisons peace. Harbored hurt hardens hearts. Jesus warned, "If ye forgive not men their trespasses, neither will your Father forgive your trespasses." (Matthew 6:15 KJV) Faith that refuses forgiveness forfeits favor. But the moment you release resentment, healing begins.

Forgiving freely doesn't mean forgetting—it means refusing to rehearse the pain. Each act of release rebuilds your emotional immunity. Stephen, while being stoned, cried out, "Lord, lay not this sin to their charge." That's perfect faith: dying to self so another can live free.

When you forgive, you imitate the cross. Every nail, every thorn, every wound whispers, "Father, forgive them." You become most like Christ when mercy wins. Perfect faith believes love can redeem even the worst offense.

Today, make forgiveness your ministry. Whoever wronged you no longer controls you. The weight you release becomes wings for your peace.

REFLECTIVE STANCE:

Who do I need to release through forgiveness today?

____

____

____

"

Forgiveness is the faith act that frees your heart for healing."
— Rev. Unnia L. Pettus, Ph.D.

PRAYER:

Lord, thank You for forgiving me completely. Give me grace to extend that same mercy to others. Heal the places that hurt and soften the memories that sting. Let love lead where anger once lived. Teach me to forgive quickly, fully, and freely. I choose release over revenge and peace over pain.
In Jesus's name, Amen.

MY FAITH NOTES FOR TODAY

____

____

____

MY FAITH DECLARATION:

I forgive freely because I've been freely forgiven.

____

____

____

DAY 35
Faith That Waits for Rain
— 1 Kings 18:41–45 —
Elijah

"And the peace of God, which passeth all understanding, shall keep your hearts and minds through Christ Jesus."
— Philippians 4:7 (KJV)

DEVOTIONAL

Perfect faith is peaceful faith. Paul wrote from a prison cell yet preached about peace that surpasses understanding. Peace doesn't mean the absence of problems—it means the presence of perspective. Faith that walks in peace keeps its composure when chaos surrounds it.

The Greek word for "keep" in this verse means "to guard like a soldier." God's peace is a military force that defends your mind from worry. When fear knocks, peace stands watch. Anxiety cannot occupy a heart already anchored in trust.

Jesus said, "Peace I leave with you." (John 14:27 KJV) That peace is not fragile; it's fortified. He carried calm into every storm. Even when winds howled, He spoke, "Peace, be still." Perfect faith echoes that authority. You can command your soul to be still because Christ lives within you.

Peace requires practice. Isaiah 26:3 promises, "Thou wilt keep him in perfect peace, whose mind is stayed on thee." Keep your mind on the Master and you'll walk through madness with stability. Meditation on Scripture re-centers the soul.

Perfect faith guards its gates. Limit negative input, increase thanksgiving. Paul said, "In everything by prayer and supplication with thanksgiving let your requests be made known unto God." Gratitude is the gate through which peace enters.

When peace rules, you respond instead of react. You become a calm within the storm. Let faith be the rudder that keeps you steady while the world spins wild.

REFLECTIVE STANCE:

What situation is God calling me to walk through in peace instead of panic?

____

____

____

"Peace isn't found in perfect circumstances but in perfect trust."
— Rev. Unnia L. Pettus, Ph.D.

PRAYER:
Father, thank You for the peace that guards my heart.
When fear rises, remind me that You reign. Teach me
to rest in Your promises and to breathe through battles.
Let Your Spirit quiet my mind and calm my emotions.
May Your peace be my portion in every place.
In Jesus's name, Amen.

MY FAITH NOTES FOR TODAY

MY FAITH DECLARATION:

I choose peace today because Christ is my calm.

DAY 36
Faith That Restores Joy
— Psalm 51:12 —
David

"We walk by faith, not by sight."
— 2 Corinthians 5:7 (KJV)

DEVOTIONAL

Perfect faith shines brightest in the dark. Anyone can believe when the path is lit, but real faith keeps walking when visibility vanishes. Abraham trusted God under a starry sky, yet still saw no heir. Job kept worshipping while sitting in ashes. Darkness is not divine absence—it is divine training.

When sight is gone, senses of the spirit awaken. Faith says, "Even here, God is still guiding." The psalmist declared, "Yea, though I walk through the valley of the shadow of death, I will fear no evil." (Psalm 23:4 KJV) The shadow proves light still exists somewhere ahead.

The night seasons of life produce revelation. In Genesis 1, God worked before dawn. Creation began in darkness, not daylight. He does His best work when you can't see it. So keep walking; dawn always follows faith's footsteps.

To trust God in the dark means letting go of the need to understand. Mary couldn't explain resurrection at the empty tomb, but she still ran to tell others. Understanding can wait; obedience cannot.

Faith also remembers that darkness develops you. Just as film is processed in darkness, so are destinies. Hidden seasons birth holy strength. Perfect faith learns to thank God not only for the sunrise but for the silence of midnight.

If you're in a dark chapter, don't close the book. The next page may contain your miracle. God is still writing.

REFLECTIVE STANCE:

Where do I need to trust God without seeing results yet?

____

____

____

"Darkness doesn't cancel God's direction; it confirms His dependability."
— Rev. Unnia L. Pettus, Ph.D.

PRAYER:

Lord, thank You for guiding me when I cannot see. Give me grace to walk by faith and not by fear. Remind me that Your presence is light enough for today. Strengthen my heart to trust in the dark. I believe You are working behind the scenes for my good.
In Jesus's name, Amen.

MY FAITH NOTES FOR TODAY

MY FAITH DECLARATION:
I trust God even in the dark because He is my light.

DAY 37
Faith That Guards the Heart
— Proverbs 4:23 —
Solomon

"Looking unto Jesus the author and finisher of our faith."
— Hebrews 12:2 (KJV)

DEVOTIONAL

Faith's focus determines faith's future. Peter walked on water until he looked at the waves. The moment his focus shifted from Christ to chaos, fear took over. Perfect faith fixes its eyes on Jesus, not the storm.

Focus is the filter that defines every moment. Life will always offer distractions—news, opinions, negativity—but faith stays centered on the Source, not the storm. Paul said, "This one thing I do." (Philippians 3:13 KJV) Focus is faith's discipline.

The enemy can't destroy you, so he tries to distract you. Every miracle requires undivided attention. When Jesus healed the blind man, He led him out of the crowd first. Sometimes God has to remove noise so you can see clearly.

Perfect faith filters what it feeds on. You can't scroll through fear and stand in faith. Set boundaries around your beliefs. Feed on Scripture, not speculation. Meditate on miracles, not mess.

To maintain focus, remember the goal is growth, not perfection. Keep your eyes on the Author and Finisher. He who started your story knows how to end it well.

Faith doesn't deny storms—it decides where to look while in them. Fix your gaze on grace, and you'll walk through waves with wonder.

REFLECTIVE STANCE:

What distractions is God asking me to remove to keep my focus on Him?

____

____

____

"Faith falters when focus fractures—keep your eyes on Jesus."

— Rev. Unnia L. Pettus, Ph.D.

PRAYER:
Lord, thank You for being the center that holds me together. Fix my eyes on Your Word when distractions call. Help me to prioritize Your presence over pressure. Guard my heart from divided focus. I choose to look to You for direction, peace, and purpose.
In Jesus's name, Amen.

MY FAITH NOTES FOR TODAY

____

____

____

MY FAITH DECLARATION:

I fix my eyes on Jesus and walk forward in faith.

____

____

____

DAY 38
Faith That Knows the Shepherd
— Psalm 23 —
David

"To obey is better than sacrifice."
— 1 Samuel 15:22 (KJV)

DEVOTIONAL

Partial obedience is still disobedience. Saul learned that lesson the hard way. God asked for complete obedience, but Saul offered convenient compromise. Perfect faith doesn't negotiate—it navigates by obedience.

When God speaks, He expects action. Noah didn't wait for raindrops before building the ark. Abraham didn't demand a map before moving. Obedience opens opportunity. Delayed obedience delays destiny.

Faith that obeys completely trusts God's instruction over human intuition. It doesn't need confirmation when command is clear. Every step of faith leads to favor.

Obedience may be costly, but it's never empty. Peter cast his net again, even after failing all night, and caught more than he imagined. Obedience turns ordinary actions into anointed moments.

Perfect faith obeys when others hesitate. It says, "If You say go, I'll go." That decision builds spiritual momentum. Each yes prepares you for the next level of assignment.

Obey God completely and watch Him complete His word in you. Faith without obedience is imagination; faith with obedience is manifestation.

REFLECTIVE STANCE:

Where is God calling me to obey completely without hesitation?

____

____

____

"Obedience is faith put to work until heaven moves on earth."

— Rev. Unnia L. Pettus, Ph.D.

PRAYER:

Lord, thank You for reminding me that obedience is better than excuses. Give me courage to follow Your voice fully. Silence doubt and strengthen my resolve to say yes without delay. Make my obedience a testimony of trust.
In Jesus's name, Amen.

MY FAITH NOTES FOR TODAY

____

____

____

MY FAITH DECLARATION:

I choose complete obedience over convenient compromise.

____

____

____

DAY 39
Faith That Wins the Battle
— 2 Chronicles 20:15 —
Jehoshaphat

"I had fainted, unless I had believed to see the goodness of the Lord in the land of the living."
— Psalm 27:13 (KJV)

DEVOTIONAL

Perfect faith expects to see goodness even in grief. David was surrounded by enemies, yet he chose to believe that God was still good. Faith sees beyond circumstances to character. It anchors itself in who God is, not what life looks like.

When your heart is heavy, train your eyes to look for light. Every new morning, every breath, every answered prayer is evidence of goodness. Psalm 23:6 declares, "Surely goodness and mercy shall follow me." Goodness doesn't chase perfect people; it chases believing ones.

Seeing goodness requires grateful vision. Complaining blinds; gratitude clarifies. When you thank God for small things, you start seeing Him in everything.

Faith that sees goodness also sees purpose in pain. Romans 8:28 reminds us that all things work together for good. Not all things feel good, but they form good. Perfect faith believes the story ends in victory.

The enemy wants to blur your view with bitterness. Shake it off. Goodness is coming behind you, mercy beside you, and grace ahead of you.

If you're still breathing, there's still beauty to behold. Open your eyes—goodness is already here.

REFLECTIVE STANCE:

Where have I seen God's goodness recently in unexpected places?

____

____

____

"Faith that looks for goodness will always find God."

— Rev. Unnia L. Pettus, Ph.D.

PRAYER:

Lord, thank You for Your unfailing goodness. Open my eyes to see Your hand in ordinary moments. Replace complaint with contentment and bitterness with belief. Even when life hurts, help me trust that Your goodness never ends.
In Jesus's name, Amen.

MY FAITH NOTES FOR TODAY

____

____

____

MY FAITH DECLARATION:

I will see God's goodness in the land of the living.

____

____

____

DAY 40
Faith That Rises Again
— Micah 7:8 —
Prophetic Resilience

"I have fought a good fight, I have finished my course, I have kept the faith."
— 2 Timothy 4:7 (KJV)

DEVOTIONAL

The goal of perfect faith isn't starting—it's finishing. Paul's final words were victory, not victimhood. He didn't boast about accomplishments; he celebrated endurance. Faith that finishes strong refuses to fade under fatigue.

Finishing faith stays focused when others fall away. It remembers that the race is not to the swift but to those who stay. (See Ecclesiastes 9 : 11.) Consistency is the true mark of maturity.

Paul endured shipwrecks, beatings, betrayal—but he kept the faith. He finished because he didn't run alone; Christ ran within him. Perfect faith knows that strength comes from the Spirit, not self.

To finish strong requires focus on eternity. Temporary troubles lose power when you see through heaven's lens. The crown awaits those who endure.

Faith that finishes strong keeps its joy. Paul sang in prison, praised under pressure, and preached while bleeding. Joy kept him fuelled when the journey felt impossible.

You may be tired, but you're too anointed to quit. The finish line is closer than you think. Run with faith until you see the Father smile.

REFLECTIVE STANCE:

What do I need to do today to finish my assignment strong?

____

____

____

"Faith doesn't just start the race—it sprints through the finish line."
— Rev. Unnia L. Pettus, Ph.D.

PRAYER:

Lord, thank You for keeping me in the race. Strengthen me to finish my course with joy. Remind me that every battle builds endurance. Help me to stay faithful until the end so my life brings You glory.
In Jesus's name, Amen.

MY FAITH NOTES FOR TODAY

____

____

____

MY FAITH DECLARATION:

I will finish strong and faithful by God's grace.

____

____

____

Days 41 ~ 50
Faith That Heals

DAY 41
Faith That Touches Jesus
— Mark 5:25–34 —
Woman With the Issue of Blood

"For God hath not given us the spirit of fear; but of power, and of love, and of a sound mind."
— 2 Timothy 1:7 (KJV)

DEVOTIONAL

Faith and fear cannot sit on the same throne of the heart. One must surrender. Paul reminded Timothy that fear is not a gift from God—it's a tactic of the enemy. Perfect faith silences fear by turning up the volume of truth.

Fear whispers, "What if?" but faith shouts, "Even if!" Daniel faced lions, David faced giants, and Esther faced death—all because courage is not the absence of fear but obedience in spite of it. When fear speaks, answer with faith's language: God is able.

Fear distorts focus. It magnifies problems and minimizes promise. Peter's fear sank him when his eyes left Jesus. Perfect faith looks beyond the storm and sees the Savior still standing.

fear knocks, let faith open the door. The Spirit inside you carries divine power, unconditional love, and stable thinking. Those three are fear's eviction notice.

Faith over fear begins with remembrance—remembering God's record. Every past victory is proof that this storm will pass too.

So, breathe deeply and declare: I will not fear. The same God who brought me through before will do it again.

REFLECTIVE STANCE:

What fear is God asking me to silence with faith today?

____

____

____

"Fear feeds on forgetting; faith flourishes on remembering."

— Rev. Unnia L. Pettus, Ph.D.

PRAYER:

Lord, thank You for replacing my fear with faith. When anxiety rises, remind me of Your power and love. Guard my mind with peace that surpasses understanding. I refuse to bow to fear; I stand in Your strength.
In Jesus's name, Amen.

MY FAITH NOTES FOR TODAY

____

____

____

MY FAITH DECLARATION:

I choose faith over fear every time.

____

____

____

DAY 42
Faith That Brings Healing Home
— Luke 7:1–10 —
Centurion's Servant

"By faith Abraham, when he was called to go out ... obeyed; and he went out, not knowing whither he went."
— Hebrews 11:8 (KJV)

DEVOTIONAL

Faith is a forward motion into mystery. Abraham left everything familiar because God said, "Go." He didn't get a GPS—he got a promise. Perfect faith moves even when the map is missing.

The unknown exposes dependence. God leads one step at a time to keep you leaning on Him. If you saw the whole route, you might try to drive alone. Faith says, "If You're with me, that's enough."

Every believer eventually faces a "Go where I send you" moment. It may be a career shift, a ministry call, or a season of surrender. The unknown is not punishment—it's promotion.

The same God who guided Abraham guides you. When He says "walk," don't wait for explanation—walk expecting manifestation.

Courage is faith's companion. The Jordan didn't part until the priests stepped in. Take the first step; God will handle the sea.

Perfect faith believes uncertainty still carries divine certainty—God is already there waiting in tomorrow.

REFLECTIVE STANCE:

Where is God calling me to walk into the unknown by faith?

____

____

____

"Faith steps into what it cannot see because it knows Who is already there."

— Rev. Unnia L. Pettus, Ph.D.

PRAYER:

Father, thank You for being my Guide in unfamiliar places. Give me the boldness to move without all the answers. When fear of the unknown tries to paralyze me, remind me that You go before me. I walk by faith into my next assignment.
In Jesus's name, Amen.

MY FAITH NOTES FOR TODAY

____

____

____

MY FAITH DECLARATION:

I walk into the unknown with confidence in God.

____

____

____

DAY 43
Faith That Calls His Name
— John 11:43–44 —
Lazarus

"Lord, I believe; help thou mine unbelief."
— Mark 9 : 24 (KJV)

DEVOTIONAL

Even strong believers battle doubt. The father of the sick boy believed—but not fully. Jesus didn't condemn him; He completed him. Perfect faith admits weakness so grace can strengthen it.

Doubt doesn't disqualify you; it draws you deeper. God can handle honesty. When you say, "Help my unbelief," you invite divine reinforcement.

Faith grows through questions answered by presence, not logic. Job never got explanations—he got revelation. Once he saw God's glory, his questions quieted.

Doubt shrinks when you rehearse what God has already done. Count past victories until fear has no room to speak.

Surround yourself with voices of faith. The paralyzed man's friends carried him to Jesus because their faith filled his gaps. Community conquers doubt.

Perfect faith may tremble, but it never quits. Keep praying through the pause until belief outweighs disbelief.

REFLECTIVE STANCE:

Where is God calling me to exchange doubt for trust?

____

____

____

"Faith isn't the absence of doubt—it's the decision to believe anyway."
— Rev. Unnia L. Pettus, Ph.D.

PRAYER:
Lord, strengthen my faith where it's weak. Replace questions with quiet confidence. When doubt tries to drown me, lift me like Peter from the waves. Remind me You've never failed. I believe and I'm becoming stronger every day.
In Jesus's name, Amen.

MY FAITH NOTES FOR TODAY

____

____

____

MY FAITH DECLARATION:

My faith is growing stronger every day.

____

____

____

DAY 44
Faith That Reaches the Roof
— Mark 2:4–5 —
Four Friends

"Be careful for nothing; but in every thing by prayer and supplication with thanksgiving let your requests be made known unto God."
— Philippians 4:6 (KJV)

DEVOTIONAL

Anxiety thrives on what-ifs; faith lives on He will. Paul knew worry firsthand, yet he taught peace in prison. Perfect faith redirects anxious energy into prayerful power.

When anxiety attacks, answer it with gratitude. Thanksgiving shifts attention from what's missing to Who's present. The antidote to worry is worship.

Prayer releases what pressure restrains. Every time you pray instead of panic, heaven trades anxiety for assurance.

Perfect faith practices perspective. What seems overwhelming is often opportunity in disguise. God's peace surpasses understanding because it guards, not just comforts.

Feed faith, starve fear. Limit what triggers worry and magnify the Word. Isaiah 26:3 promises perfect peace for minds stayed on God.

Faith doesn't ignore reality; it invites divine authority over it. Declare peace even while shaking—your confession creates calm.

REFLECTIVE STANCE:

Which worry do I need to turn into worship today?

____

____

____

"Anxiety evaporates where adoration abides."

— Rev. Unnia L. Pettus, Ph.D.

PRAYER:

Father, thank You for peace that passes understanding. When I feel overwhelmed, remind me to pray instead of panic. Fill my heart with gratitude that pushes worry away. I cast my cares on You because You care for me. In Jesus's name, Amen.

MY FAITH NOTES FOR TODAY

MY FAITH DECLARATION:
Peace is my portion because God is in control.

DAY 45
Faith That Rises From the Bed
— Mark 2:11–12 —
Paralyzed Man

"Be not afraid of their faces: for I am with thee to deliver thee, saith the Lord."
— Jeremiah 1:8 (KJV)

DEVOTIONAL

When God called Jeremiah, the young prophet trembled. He felt unqualified, unheard, and afraid of people's opinions. But God silenced every fearful voice with one promise: "I am with you." Perfect faith listens to that voice above all others.

Fearful voices say, "You can't." Faithful voices declare, "God can." Every great assignment comes with opposition. The measure of your calling often matches the noise of your critics.

Perfect faith learns to stand tall even when surrounded by doubt. David heard Goliath roar, but remembered God's record. Faith tunes its ear to the divine frequency of truth.

You don't need everyone's approval—just God's anointing. When you walk in divine purpose, human opinion becomes background noise.

Courage comes when conviction outweighs criticism. The fire of your faith burns louder than the fear of rejection.

Stand up, speak out, and trust that the God who called you will cover you. Your voice carries heaven's authority.

REFLECTIVE STANCE:
Whose voice do I need to ignore to follow God's assignment?

____

____

____

"Faith turns down fear's volume to hear God's voice clearly."
— Rev. Unnia L. Pettus, Ph.D.

PRAYER:
Lord, thank You for reminding me that You're with me. Silence the voices of doubt that try to diminish my confidence. Let Your Word be the loudest sound in my soul. I will speak, serve, and stand without fear because You go before me.
In Jesus's name, Amen.

MY FAITH NOTES FOR TODAY

____

____

____

MY FAITH DECLARATION:
I defy fear by listening to God's voice alone.

____

____

____

DAY 46
Faith That Walks Again
— John 5:8 —
Bethesda Healing

"For verily I say unto you, That whosoever shall say unto this mountain, Be thou removed, and be thou cast into the sea; and shall not doubt in his heart, but shall believe that those things which he saith shall come to pass; he shall have whatsoever he saith."
— Mark 11 : 23 (KJV)

DEVOTIONAL

Faith that moves mountains begins with a mouth that moves in agreement with God. Jesus spoke these words after cursing the fig tree—He demonstrated that authority flows from alignment. Perfect faith understands that mountains move when your belief and your confession meet.

The mountain is anything that blocks your progress: fear, debt, sickness, rejection, doubt, shame. Mountains look big until you remember the size of your God. David faced a towering Goliath, but his confidence wasn't in stones—it was in the Lord of hosts. Faith doesn't ignore the mountain; it instructs it.

Mountains move when we speak with conviction. Too often we describe our problems to God instead of declaring His promises to the problem. Joshua watched Jericho's walls fall after Israel marched and shouted. Your faith may not need another meeting—it may need a mouthful of Scripture.

Perfect faith refuses to partner with doubt. Jesus said, "Shall not doubt in his heart." Doubt divides belief; faith unifies it. A double-minded person prays but panics, believes but complains. Faith says, "I believe until I see it, and when I see it, I'll still believe more."

Mountain-moving faith also remembers timing. Sometimes God moves the mountain instantly; other times He gives you strength to climb it. Either way, His power prevails. Moses didn't bulldoze the Red Sea—he stretched his staff and watched God part it. Your obedience opens the path.

Faith that moves mountains starts with relationship. The more time you spend in God's presence, the more authority fills your prayers. The closer you walk with the Creator, the less you fear creation.

REFLECTIVE STANCE:
What "mountain" in my life needs me to speak God's Word over it today?

____

____

____

"Mountains don't move because you shout —
they move because you believe. "
— Rev. Unnia L. Pettus, Ph.D.

PRAYER:
Lord, thank You for giving me power through faith-filled words. Strengthen my belief so doubt loses its grip. Teach me to speak Your promises with boldness. Let every obstacle yield to Your authority working in me. I trust that every mountain must move at Your command.
In Jesus's name, Amen.

MY FAITH NOTES FOR TODAY

____

____

____

MY FAITH DECLARATION:
I will speak God's Word until mountains move and miracles manifest.

____

____

____

DAY 47
Faith That Breaks Chains
— Acts 12:7 —
Peter in Prison

"And Moses said unto the people, Fear ye not, standstill, and see the salvation of the Lord, which he will shew to you today."
— Exodus 14 : 13 (KJV)

DEVOTIONAL

Standing still in faith doesn't mean doing nothing—it means doing the most important thing: trusting. Israel had the Red Sea before them and Pharaoh behind them. Panic seemed logical, but God's command was radical: "Stand still." Perfect faith holds its position when everything screams "run."

Standing still means stability in the storm. The sea did not part until the people stopped complaining. Miracles manifest where movement meets stillness— where human effort pauses so divine power can perform.

Stillness is spiritual strength. Psalm 46 : 10 reminds us, "Be still, and know that I am God." The Hebrew word for still means "to let go." Faith lets go of control so grace can take over.

When life pressures you to act in haste, faith whispers, "Wait." Waiting is warfare that confuses the enemy. He expects panic, not patience.

The Israelites saw salvation when they stood still long enough for God to show Himself mighty. Sometimes your assignment isn't to fight; it's to be still and watch God work.

Perfect faith doesn't flinch at Pharaoh or fear the flood—it stands still and sees salvation unfold.

REFLECTIVE STANCE:

Where is God asking me to stop striving and stand still in trust?

____

____

____

"Stillness is not surrender—it's strategy."
— Rev. Unnia L. Pettus, Ph.D.

PRAYER:

Father, teach me the strength of stillness. When fear tempts me to rush, remind me You fight for me. I release control and rest in Your timing. Let me witness Your salvation in my situation.
In Jesus's name, Amen.

MY FAITH NOTES FOR TODAY

____

____

____

MY FAITH DECLARATION:
I will stand still and watch God work wonders.

____

____

____

DAY 48
Faith That Restores Sight
— Mark 10:46–52 —
Bartimaeus

"Death and life are in the power of the tongue: and they that love it shall eat the fruit thereof."
— Proverbs 18 : 21 (KJV)

DEVOTIONAL

Words create worlds. God spoke light into darkness and breathed life into dust. You, made in His image, carry that same creative authority. Perfect faith speaks life even when life looks lifeless.

Ezekiel stood in a valley full of dry bones. God asked, "Can these bones live?" The prophet answered wisely, "O Lord God, thou knowest." Then God said, "Prophesy to these bones." Faith talks resurrection language.

Every declaration shapes destiny. If you constantly say, "I'll never make it," your faith starves. Speak possibility, not pessimism. Replace, "I'm broke," with, "My God shall supply all my need."

Jesus spoke to Lazarus's tomb and death obeyed. When He said, "Lazarus, come forth," the grave had to release what it held. That's the same authority you carry when you speak in alignment with heaven.

Speaking life is not denial—it's divine determination. You're calling things that are not as though they were because you trust the God who can make them so.

Let your words water the seeds of your faith. Speak healing, hope, and holiness until your situation looks like your declaration.

REFLECTIVE STANCE:

What negative confession do I need to replace with life-giving words today?

____

____

____

"Speak what God said, not what fear shows."

— Rev. Unnia L. Pettus, Ph.D.

PRAYER:

Lord, bridle my tongue with truth. Let every word I speak carry grace and faith. Forgive careless words that have planted doubt. Teach me to decree life over every circumstance. I declare victory, healing, and abundance in Your name.

In Jesus's name, Amen.

MY FAITH NOTES FOR TODAY

____

____

____

MY FAITH DECLARATION:
My words align with God's Word; I speak life only.

____

____

____

DAY 49
Faith That Receives Mercy
— Luke 17:12–19 —
Ten Lepers

"They that wait upon the Lord shall renew their strength; they shall mount up with wings as eagles; they shall run, and not be weary; and they shall walk, and not faint."
— Isaiah 40:31 (KJV)

DEVOTIONAL

Waiting is one of faith's hardest tests. We want microwaves; God prefers marination. Perfect faith waits well because it trusts who is coming even when it can't see when.

Waiting well means worshiping while you wait. The Hebrew word for wait means "to twist or bind together." When you wait on God, you entwine your strength with His. That's why you rise like eagles—because you're flying on divine wind.

Abraham waited twenty-five years for Isaac. Joseph waited thirteen years for his dream. Jesus waited thirty years for His public ministry. Waiting isn't wasted when you walk with God.

Faithful waiting builds endurance. The cocoon is uncomfortable, but it produces wings. Every delay refines your character for destiny.

While you wait, watch your words. Don't curse the calendar. Declare, "My due season is on schedule." Faith doesn't whine about timing; it worships the Timeless One.

God's promises aren't late—they're loading. Every prayer sown in patience will bloom in perfect time.

REFLECTIVE STANCE:

Where is God asking me to wait with worship instead of worry?

____

____

____

"Delay isn't denial—it's divine development."

— Rev. Unnia L. Pettus, Ph.D.

Prayer:
Lord, thank You for reminding me that waiting is working. Help me to trust Your timing when my heart grows restless. Renew my strength like the eagle's. Teach me to sing through the silence and praise in the pause. I believe my season is on schedule.
In Jesus's name, Amen.

MY FAITH NOTES FOR TODAY

MY FAITH DECLARATION:
I wait well, knowing God's timing is perfect.

DAY 50
Faith That Heals the Heart
— Psalm 147:3 —
Healing from Brokenness

"While we look not at the things which are seen, but at the things which are not seen: for the things which are seen are temporal; but the things which are not seen are eternal."
— 2 Corinthians 4:18 (KJV)

DEVOTIONAL

Faith sees beyond facts. It looks at the unseen and calls it reality. Perfect faith wears heaven's glasses—it perceives promise through pain.

Elisha's servant panicked when surrounded by enemies, but the prophet prayed, "Lord, open his eyes." Suddenly the servant saw chariots of fire around them. The unseen army was always there; faith simply revealed it.

Seeing the invisible requires spiritual vision sharpened by Scripture. The more you meditate on God's Word, the clearer unseen truth becomes.

Faith sees victory before it happens. Noah saw rain before it fell. Mary saw resurrection before it came. Vision born in faith becomes manifestation in time.

Perfect faith refuses to be defined by what eyes can measure. It believes that the invisible hand of God is rearranging everything visible for His glory.

What you see determines how you stand. Keep your eyes fixed on eternity—where every unseen promise is already finished in God's plan.

REFLECTIVE STANCE:
What invisible promise is God asking me to see with faith's eyes today?

____

____

____

"Faith doesn't wait to see to believe—it believes to see."
— Rev. Unnia L. Pettus, Ph.D.

Prayer:
Father, open my spiritual eyes to see Your hand at work. When circumstances cloud my vision, remind me that faith sees differently. Let my focus rest on what is eternal, not temporary. I believe what You've promised will come to pass.
In Jesus's name, Amen.

MY FAITH NOTES FOR TODAY

____

____

____

MY FAITH DECLARATION:
I see the invisible and believe the impossible.

____

____

____

Days 51 ~ 60
Faith That Endures

DAY 51
Faith That Holds On
— Genesis 22:8 —
Abraham and Isaac

"And he arose, and rebuked the wind, and said unto the sea, Peace, be still. And the wind ceased, and there was a great calm."
— Mark 4 : 39 (KJV)

DEVOTIONAL

Faith that endures isn't proven in sunshine; it's perfected in storms. The disciples followed Jesus into a boat, only to face fierce winds that threatened their safety. Even with Jesus onboard, the storm still came. Perfect faith understands that proximity to Christ doesn't prevent trouble—it promises triumph.

The sea roared, waves rose, and fear gripped their hearts. They shouted, "Master, carest thou not that we perish?" Yet the same Jesus asleep in the stern was Lord over the storm. When He spoke, creation obeyed. Faith that endures learns to rest where He rests, not react how fear reacts.

Every believer will face seasons when the winds howl louder than their worship. In those moments, remember: storms don't come to drown you—they come to deepen you. Each wave is a classroom teaching trust.

Faith endures when we focus on the Word, not the wind. The storm didn't surprise Jesus; He planned it to show His power. The same Savior who said, "Let us go to the other side," ensured they'd make it. If He said go, you can't sink.

Perfect faith sees beyond the chaos to the calm already written in heaven. You may bend, but you won't break. The wind will stop, but your worship must not.

When the waves of life rage, rest your head on the same pillow Jesus did—peace rooted in promise.

REFLECTIVE STANCE:

What storm am I learning to rest through rather than react to?

____

____

____

"Faith doesn't stop storms; it stills the soul while they rage."
— Rev. Unnia L. Pettus, Ph.D.

Prayer:
Lord, thank You for being peace in my storm. When I panic, remind me that You're still present and powerful. Calm my thoughts, quiet my fears, and let my faith rise above the waves. Teach me to rest in Your sovereignty. In Jesus's name, Amen.

MY FAITH NOTES FOR TODAY

____

____

____

MY FAITH DECLARATION:
I am calm in the storm because Christ is in my boat.

____

____

____

DAY 52
Faith That Learns to Let Go
— Ruth 1:16–17 —
Ruth and Naomi

"Though it tarry, wait for it; because it will surely come,
it will not tarry."
— Habakkuk 2:3 (KJV)

DEVOTIONAL

Waiting seasons test endurance like no other. Habakkuk cried for answers, and heaven seemed silent. Yet God reminded him, the vision has an appointed time. Perfect faith endures waiting because it trusts divine timing more than human impatience.

God's delays are not His denials; they're developmental. Waiting grows spiritual muscle. David was anointed as king but served in obscurity for years. Joseph dreamed of leadership but endured prison before promotion.

Faith that endures waiting knows heaven's clock never runs late. The Hebrew word for "wait" in Isaiah 40:31 means "to bind together." As you wait, your spirit intertwines with God's. That's why the weary are renewed.

When impatience rises, remember that fruit ripens best in season. Rushed blessings spoil; cultivated ones satisfy.

Perfect faith keeps working while waiting. Noah kept building though rain hadn't come. Faith keeps moving even when manifestation feels miles away.

Every delay has purpose—to protect, prepare, or prove you. The waiting room of faith is where winners are shaped.

REFLECTIVE STANCE:
Where am I tempted to rush God's timing instead of resting in it?

____

____

____

"Faith doesn't fold in the waiting; it grows roots."

— Rev. Unnia L. Pettus, Ph.D.

Prayer:
Father, thank You for teaching me patience in delay. Help me trust Your pace even when I don't see progress. Strengthen me to wait with worship, not worry. I believe what You promised is on schedule. In Jesus's name, Amen.

MY FAITH NOTES FOR TODAY

____

____

____

MY FAITH DECLARATION:
I wait well because my faith is rooted in God's timing.

____

____

____

DAY 53
Faith That Rises From Disappointment
— Luke 24:32 —
Emmaus Disciples

"The stone which the builders refused is become the head stone of the corner."
— Psalm 118:22 (KJV)

DEVOTIONAL

Rejection hurts, but it refines. Perfect faith knows that being refused by man often means being reserved by God. Joseph's brothers sold him out, but God used it to set him up. Rejection redirected him into destiny.

Faith that endures rejection refuses bitterness. It sees every "no" as God's way of saying, "I have better." Jesus Himself was despised and rejected of men (Isaiah 53 : 3), yet that rejection became redemption.

When people push you aside, remember heaven still holds your place. Faith whispers, "Even this will work for good." (Romans 8 : 28)

Rejection reveals resilience. David was overlooked by Samuel but chosen by God. Man's opinion doesn't override divine ordination.

Perfect faith transforms wounds into worship. Every betrayal becomes the birthplace of breakthrough. God uses dismissal as direction.

Don't chase those who walked away; chase the One who's calling you forward. Rejection isn't your ending—it's your elevation.

REFLECTIVE STANCE:

Where has rejection redirected me closer to God's purpose?

____

____

____

"Rejection is often God's redirection toward revelation."
— Rev. Unnia L. Pettus, Ph.D.

Prayer:
Lord, thank You for every closed door that led me to open grace. Heal the places rejection wounded me. Remind me that Your approval outweighs every earthly denial. Strengthen my faith to see purpose in the pain. In Jesus's name, Amen.

MY FAITH NOTES FOR TODAY

MY FAITH DECLARATION:
Rejection refines me; God's approval defines me.

DAY 54
Faith That Walks Through Fire
— Isaiah 43:2 —
Three Hebrew Boys

"Knowing this, that the trying of your faith worketh patience."
— James 1:3 (KJV)

DEVOTIONAL

Every test of faith is a trust exercise. Trials aren't proof of God's absence—they're invitations to prove His strength. James encourages believers to count it all joy because testing develops endurance.

Abraham's faith was tested on Mount Moriah when God asked for Isaac. Yet his obedience birthed a generational blessing. Perfect faith obeys even when it doesn't understand.

Tests expose what's real. Anyone can worship in abundance; true faith praises in affliction. Job's testimony still echoes, "Though He slay me, yet will I trust Him."

Faith tested becomes faith trusted. Gold must go through fire before it shines. Testing removes impurities that hinder belief.

When life feels like a classroom with no teacher visible, remember—the Instructor is silent during the test. But He's watching your endurance become excellence.

Perfect faith endures because it knows storms sharpen spiritual skill. You'll come out stronger, wiser, and more grounded than before.

REFLECTIVE STANCE:

What current test is God using to strengthen my patience?

____

____

____

"Tests are temporary teachers shaping permanent trust."

— Rev. Unnia L. Pettus, Ph.D.

Prayer:

Father, thank You for turning my tests into testimonies. When pressure mounts, keep me steady. Let patience have her perfect work in me. Make my faith unshakable through every trial.
In Jesus's name, Amen.

MY FAITH NOTES FOR TODAY

MY FAITH DECLARATION:
Every test becomes my testimony of triumph.

DAY 55
Faith That Overcomes Fear
— Psalm 27:1 —
David

"The Lord gave, and the Lord hath taken away; blessed be the name of the Lord."
— Job 1:21 (KJV)

DEVOTIONAL

Loss tests faith like little else. Job lost wealth, health, and family—but not worship. Perfect faith doesn't praise God because of possessions; it praises Him in spite of loss.

Faith that endures loss understands that life shifts but God stays. Seasons change, but sovereignty doesn't. Job's faith wasn't built on circumstance—it was anchored in character.

Enduring loss means trusting that God's plan still includes your peace. Joseph lost his coat but not his calling. Ruth lost her husband but found redemption.

Grief is real, but grace is greater. God never wastes pain; He repurposes it. Every loss becomes the seed of later laughter.

Perfect faith says, "Even if I lose everything, I still have Jesus." And that's enough.

When your hands feel empty, lift them anyway. Worship fills the void with wonder.

REFLECTIVE STANCE:
How has loss taught me to depend more deeply on God's presence?

____

____

____

"Faith doesn't deny pain—it discovers purpose within it."
— Rev. Unnia L. Pettus, Ph.D.

Prayer:
Lord, thank You for being my constant when life shifts. Heal my heart and hold my hope. Help me bless Your name through tears. Let every loss birth new life within me.
In Jesus's name, Amen.

MY FAITH NOTES FOR TODAY

MY FAITH DECLARATION:

Even in loss, I am loved, and my faith still stands.

DAY 56
Faith That Waits in the Valley
— Psalm 23:4 —
David

"For the vision is yet for an appointed time, but at the end it shall speak, and not lie: though it tarry, wait for it; because it will surely come, it will not tarry."
— Habakkuk 2:3 (KJV)

DEVOTIONAL

Delay is not defeat; it's divine discipline for destiny. Perfect faith learns that God's clock runs on kingdom time, not human calendars. Abraham waited twenty-five years for Isaac, Hannah prayed for years before Samuel was born, and Joseph endured thirteen years before his dream stepped into daylight. Delay develops endurance, and endurance deepens trust.

In the space between promise and performance, heaven trains your heart. If God gave you everything too early, the blessing might break you. Delay builds durability—faith muscles strengthened by waiting. David wrote psalms in caves before he ever sat on a throne; his delay taught him dependence.

Faith that endures delay worships while waiting. Praise is not a reward after fulfillment; it's preparation before manifestation. When Paul and Silas sang in prison, the walls shook. Delay cannot chain a believer who knows how to praise.

God's "not yet" is still a "yes" in process. Habakkuk reminds us that the vision will speak. While you wonder if God forgot, He's aligning people, places, and purpose.

When delay tempts you to doubt, rehearse what He's already done. Yesterday's testimonies sustain today's tension.

Perfect faith doesn't ask when but declares Who: "My God will show up on time."

REFLECTIVE STANCE:
How can I honor God with my attitude while I wait?

____

____

____

"Delay is heaven's way of preparing you for the weight of destiny."
— Rev. Unnia L. Pettus, Ph.D.

PRAYER:

Lord, thank You for every waiting room that refines my worship. Teach me patience when progress seems paused. Let my hope rest in Your timing, not my timeline. Strengthen me to praise while I wait, knowing delay is development.
In Jesus's name, Amen.

MY FAITH NOTES FOR TODAY

____

____

____

MY FAITH DECLARATION:

I trust God's timing even when the clock feels slow.

____

____

____

DAY 57
Faith That Climbs Higher
— Luke 19:4–5 —
Zacchaeus

"We are troubled on every side, yet not distressed; we are perplexed, but not in despair."
— 2 Corinthians 4:8 (KJV)

DEVOTIONAL

Disappointment is the intersection where expectation meets experience. Paul knew that place well—imprisoned, betrayed, shipwrecked—yet his faith endured. Perfect faith refuses to let temporary pain rewrite eternal promises.

Every disappointment hides divine appointment. When Samuel mourned Saul's failure, God said, "How long wilt thou mourn for Saul? ... fill thine horn with oil, and go." (1 Samuel 16:1 KJV) Disappointment signals it's time for new direction.

Faith that endures disappointment transforms tears into tools. Joseph's betrayal built the bridge to Egypt. Peter's denial birthed deeper devotion. God never wastes brokenness; He rebuilds it better.

When life lets you down, lift your eyes up. Hope is a holy habit. Isaiah 61 : 3 promises beauty for ashes—the trade-in policy of heaven.

Perfect faith doesn't pretend pain away; it prays through it. Cry, but don't quit. Mourn, but move. God specializes in turning "why" into "wow."

Disappointment may close one door, but faith reminds you another has already been opened.

REFLECTIVE STANCE:

What past disappointment is God turning into direction for me?

____

____

____

"Disappointment is destiny's detour, not its death."

— Rev. Unnia L. Pettus, Ph.D.

PRAYER:

Father, thank You for meeting me in my disappointments. Heal my heart where hope has been bruised. Teach me to see Your hand rewriting my story for good. Let resilience rise where regret once lived. In Jesus's name, Amen.

MY FAITH NOTES FOR TODAY

MY FAITH DECLARATION:
My faith outlasts every disappointment.

DAY 58
Faith That Overcomes Doubt
— John 20:27–29 —
Thomas

"There hath no temptation taken you but such as is common to man: but God is faithful, who will not suffer you to be tempted above that ye are able; but will with the temptation also make a way to escape."
— 1 Corinthians 10:13 (KJV)

DEVOTIONAL

Temptation tests loyalty. The enemy tempts to destroy; God allows it to strengthen. Perfect faith learns to resist because it remembers. Jesus faced Satan in the wilderness but defeated him with "It is written."

Faith that endures temptation chooses covenant over convenience. Joseph fled Potiphar's wife because his relationship with God mattered more than momentary pleasure. Running from sin isn't weakness—it's wisdom.

Temptation often comes dressed as opportunity. It whispers shortcuts to destiny. But faith stays patient, knowing premature promotion can sabotage purpose.

The way of escape is always there—sometimes a verse, sometimes a door, sometimes silence. Stay sensitive. The Spirit that sealed you will steer you.

Perfect faith sees temptation not as humiliation but as invitation to prove faithfulness. Every time you resist, you reveal Christ's strength in you.

Victory isn't never being tempted; it's consistently choosing truth over traps.

REFLECTIVE STANCE:
What escape route has God given me that I must choose today?

____

____

____

"Faith faces temptation not with pride but with power."
— Rev. Unnia L. Pettus, Ph.D.

PRAYER:
Lord, thank You for being faithful in my weakness. Strengthen me to choose righteousness when temptation calls. Let Your Word be my weapon and Your Spirit my guide. Remind me I am more than a conqueror through You.
In Jesus's name, Amen.

MY FAITH NOTES FOR TODAY

____

____

____

MY FAITH DECLARATION:

I overcome temptation through God's power within me.

____

____

____

DAY 59
Faith That Never Fails
— Luke 22:32 —
Peter

"When my father and my mother forsake me, then the Lord will take me up."
— Psalm 27:10 (KJV)

DEVOTIONAL

Loneliness is one of faith's secret classrooms. Even Jesus experienced it—forsaken by friends in Gethsemane. Perfect faith learns that solitude is not abandonment; it's appointment.

When everyone else leaves, God draws near. In isolation, revelation increases. John wrote the Book of Revelation alone on Patmos. Moses met God alone on Sinai. Some glory is only seen in solitude.

Faith that endures loneliness transforms absence into intimacy. Instead of asking, "Who left?" ask, "Who stayed?" The answer will always be—God.

Loneliness sharpens spiritual hearing. When the crowd quiets, the Comforter speaks. Elijah heard God not in the wind or earthquake, but in the still small voice.

Perfect faith stops chasing company and starts cherishing communion. The presence of the Lord fills every empty space.

Loneliness may visit, but it cannot live where faith resides.

REFLECTIVE STANCE:
How is God using solitude to strengthen my relationship with Him?

____

____

____

"Loneliness becomes holy when you realize you're never alone."
— Rev. Unnia L. Pettus, Ph.D.

PRAYER:
Father, thank You for meeting me in lonely places. Fill my heart with Your presence. Teach me to find joy in You when others walk away. Turn isolation into inspiration. I am never alone because You dwell within me.
In Jesus's name, Amen.

MY FAITH NOTES FOR TODAY

____

____

____

MY FAITH DECLARATION:
God's presence fills every empty place in my life.

____

____

____

DAY 60
Faith That Finishes Strong
— 2 Timothy 4:7 —
Paul

"To every thing there is a season, and a time to every purpose under the heaven."
— Ecclesiastes 3:1 (KJV)

DEVOTIONAL

Faith that endures every season is faith that adapts without abandoning belief. Life shifts through spring's growth, summer's harvest, autumn's pruning, and winter's waiting—but God remains constant.

Abraham endured barren seasons before blessing. David faced both palace applause and cave isolation. Paul preached through shipwreck and success. Perfect faith doesn't depend on the weather; it depends on the Word.

Every season serves a purpose. The cold builds character; the heat tests endurance. You can't curse the season that cultivates your calling.

Faith that endures learns contentment. Paul declared, "I have learned, in whatsoever state I am, therewith to be content." (Philippians 4 : 11 KJV)

Contentment is courage to trust God's wisdom in timing.

When the season feels harsh, remember the Gardener knows what He's growing. Even pruning is preparation for fruitfulness.

Perfect faith endures because it's rooted in the unchanging One. Seasons pass, but the Savior never does.

REFLECTIVE STANCE:
Which season am I in, and what is God teaching me through it?

____

____

____

"Faith doesn't fear seasons—it flourishes in all of them."
— Rev. Unnia L. Pettus, Ph.D.

PRAYER:
Lord, thank You for being faithful in every season. Teach me to embrace change without complaint. Let my roots go deep so my faith stays steady through storms and sunshine. I trust the process and praise You for purpose in every phase.
In Jesus's name, Amen.

MY FAITH NOTES FOR TODAY

MY FAITH DECLARATION:
My faith flourishes in every season of life.

Days 61 – 70
Faith That Overcomes Adversity

DAY 61
Faith That Endures the Fire
— Isaiah 43:2 —
Shadrach, Meshach & Abednego

"When thou walkest through the fire, thou shalt not be burned; neither shall the flame kindle upon thee."
— Isaiah 43:2 (KJV)

DEVOTIONAL

Fire either destroys or refines depending on what it finds. Perfect faith understands that fiery trials are not meant to consume but to confirm. The three Hebrew boys—Shadrach, Meshach, and Abednego—refused to bow before Babylon's golden image. When thrown into the furnace, they met a fourth man walking beside them. Fire reveals fellowship; flames prove faithfulness.

Faith that endures the fire doesn't compromise to avoid conflict. The boys told the king, "Our God whom we serve is able to deliver us, and He will deliver us... but if not, we will not bow." That's perfect faith—bold enough to believe for deliverance but anchored enough to trust even if it doesn't come.

God didn't keep them from the fire; He joined them in it. His presence changed the purpose of the flames. The same heat that killed their captors became the catalyst for their promotion. Every fiery trial you face refines your purpose and exposes His power.

Fire burns what binds. The Scripture says their ropes fell off, but not a hair was singed. Sometimes you must walk through heat so that bondage can burn away.

When faith endures the furnace, the testimony echoes through generations. Nebuchadnezzar declared, "There is no other god that can deliver after this sort."

Your fire will not destroy you; it will distinguish you.

REFLECTIVE STANCE:

What "fire" in my life is God using to refine my faith right now?

____

____

____

"The fire that should have finished you will forge you for greater faith."
— Rev. Unnia L. Pettus, Ph.D.

PRAYER:
Lord, thank You for being with me in every flame. When life feels heated, remind me You are my protection and purpose. Let what's burned away be everything that blocks my belief. I trust that what I face will only make my faith purer.
In Jesus's name, Amen.

MY FAITH NOTES FOR TODAY

____

____

____

MY FAITH DECLARATION:
I will not bow in the fire; I will believe in the flame.

____

____

____

DAY 62
Faith That Overcomes Fear
— Psalm 27:1 —
David

"The Lord is my light and my salvation; whom shall I fear?"
— Psalm 27:1 (KJV)

DEVOTIONAL

Fear feeds on imagination, but faith focuses on illumination. David wrote Psalm 27 surrounded by enemies yet shining with confidence. Perfect faith recognizes that fear may knock, but courage answers.

When fear whispers, "You can't," faith replies, "The Lord already did." Gideon hid from his enemies until God called him a mighty man of valor. The title preceded the transformation. Faith accepts identity before evidence.

Fear paralyzes; faith mobilizes. Israel trembled before Goliath, but David ran toward him. What made the difference? Perspective. Fear looked at Goliath compared to self; faith looked at Goliath compared to God.

Faith that overcomes fear learns to worship louder than worry. Paul and Silas sang in prison while chains clanged around them. Worship shifts focus from threat to throne.

Perfect faith feeds courage daily through prayer, Scripture, and remembrance. Every past victory becomes a sword against current fear.

Fear loses its grip where God's light shines. Turn your face toward Him—the shadows can't follow where glory dwells.

REFLECTIVE STANCE:
Where is fear still trying to silence my faith?

____

____

____

"Fear shrinks when faith speaks."
— Rev. Unnia L. Pettus, Ph.D.

PRAYER:
*Father, thank You for being my light in dark seasons. When fear rises, let faith roar. Teach me to see challenges as opportunities to trust You more. I choose courage over comfort and worship over worry.
In Jesus's name, Amen.*

MY FAITH NOTES FOR TODAY

____

____

____

MY FAITH DECLARATION:
I fear no evil because faith is my foundation.

____

____

____

DAY 63
Faith That Walks in Peace
— Philippians 4:7 —
Paul

"Yea, mine own familiar friend, in whom I trusted, which did eat of my bread, hath lifted up his heel against me."
— Psalm 41:9 (KJV)

DEVOTIONAL

Few wounds cut deeper than betrayal. David wrote these words about a close friend; Jesus lived them through Judas. Perfect faith learns to love even through betrayal because it looks beyond the betrayer to the bigger picture.

Betrayal doesn't surprise God; it serves Him. Judas's kiss led to Calvary, and Calvary led to resurrection. Sometimes the hand that hurts you is the hinge that opens destiny's door.

Faith that endures betrayal refuses bitterness. Joseph forgave brothers who sold him into slavery, saying, "Ye thought evil against me; but God meant it unto good." Forgiveness frees faith to flourish.

Every betrayal births a blessing if you handle it with grace. Let pain push you to prayer, not revenge.

Perfect faith also recognizes patterns. Jesus called Judas "friend" even at the moment of deceit. True strength is kindness that outlasts cruelty.

When betrayed, remember: you're in good company. The Savior understands.

REFLECTIVE STANCE:

How can I turn betrayal into a bridge for growth rather than bitterness?

____

____

____

"Betrayal becomes breakthrough when you keep your heart clean."
— Rev. Unnia L. Pettus, Ph.D.

PRAYER:

Lord, thank You for healing betrayal's sting. Guard my heart from bitterness. Teach me to release revenge and embrace redemption. Use every wound to draw me nearer to You. I forgive as You forgave me.
In Jesus's name, Amen.

MY FAITH NOTES FOR TODAY

____

____

____

MY FAITH DECLARATION:
I rise above betrayal with grace and forgiveness.

____

____

____

DAY 64
Faith That Climbs the Mountain
— Exodus 19:3 —
Moses on Mount Sinai

"Many are the afflictions of the righteous: but the Lord deliravereth him out of them all."
— Psalm 34:19 (KJV)

DEVOTIONAL

Adversity is not absence—it's assignment. Perfect faith expects opposition because purpose provokes it. David wrote these words after fleeing Saul, hiding in caves yet still trusting in deliverance.

Faith that endures adversity finds assurance in "out of them all." God doesn't promise a life without trouble, but He promises triumph through it.
Adversity sharpens awareness. In pressure, you see provision clearer. Elijah found sustenance by a brook and a widow's hand only when drought hit.

Faith doesn't flinch under fire; it flourishes. The more life squeezes you, the more anointing flows if you remain rooted. Paul's imprisonment produced epistles; adversity birthed advancement.

Perfect faith sees adversity as assignment—training for elevation. Giants exist to reveal giant-killers. Endurance is evidence that grace is active. You're still standing because faith fortified you.

REFLECTIVE STANCE:
How is God using my adversity as an assignment for growth?

____

____

____

"Adversity exposes anointing."
— Rev. Unnia L. Pettus, Ph.D.

PRAYER:
Lord, thank You for deliverance in every adversity.
Remind me that affliction cannot cancel anointing.
Give me courage to see tests as training. Strengthen my
faith until triumph testifies.
In Jesus's name, Amen.

MY FAITH NOTES FOR TODAY

____

____

____

MY FAITH DECLARATION:

I am anointed to overcome every adversity.

____

____

____

DAY 65
Faith That Wins in the Wilderness
— Deuteronomy 8:2 —
Israel Tested and Taught

"David encouraged himself in the Lord his God."
— 1 Samuel 30:6 (KJV)

DEVOTIONAL

Encouragement is not always external; sometimes it must be internal. At Ziklag, David lost everything—family, home, followers' loyalty—but not faith. Perfect faith finds courage in communion with God when comfort from people disappears.

Discouragement drains energy, but faith restores it through remembrance. David strengthened himself by recalling past victories: the lion, the bear, the giant. Remembrance revives resilience.

Faith that overcomes discouragement learns to talk to the soul. Psalm 42:5 says, "Why art thou cast down, O my soul? hope thou in God." Speak hope until heart follows.

Encouragement is spiritual warfare. The enemy wins when you stay silent; he loses when you worship.

Perfect faith praises in pain, prays under pressure, and perseveres through panic. Every "still standing" moment becomes a song of survival.

Lift your head, child of God. The same Lord who restored David will renew you.

REFLECTIVE STANCE:
What words of encouragement is God whispering to my spirit today?

____

____

____

"When no one else cheers you on, heaven still claps."

— Rev. Unnia L. Pettus, Ph.D.

PRAYER:
Father, thank You for strength in solitude. Teach me to encourage myself with Your Word. Restore my joy where weariness has weighed me down. I lift my eyes to You, my source of strength.
In Jesus's name, Amen.

MY FAITH NOTES FOR TODAY

MY FAITH DECLARATION:
I will stay encouraged because God is still in control.

DAY 66
Faith That Rests in the Promise
— Hebrews 4:9 —
Believers' Rest in God

"Yea, and all that will live godly in Christ Jesus shall suffer persecution."
— 2 Timothy 3 : 12 (KJV)

DEVOTIONAL

Faith that endures persecution stands when pressured to bow. The early church was hunted, whipped, and imprisoned, yet the gospel grew stronger. Perfect faith understands that opposition authenticates obedience—if no one resists your light, maybe you're hiding it.

Paul wrote Timothy this warning while chained in Rome, not from fear but from fire. Persecution doesn't prove failure; it proves you're carrying truth the world can't tolerate. The same flames that sought to silence believers became the torch that lit generations.

When you face ridicule for righteousness, rejoice—heaven records it. Jesus said, "Blessed are ye when men shall revile you." Faith doesn't need applause; it seeks approval from the Almighty.

Perfect faith doesn't retaliate—it radiates. Stephen forgave his killers as stones flew. That moment planted the seed for Paul's conversion. Every persecuted believer becomes proof that love outlasts hate.

In this age, persecution may look like isolation, cancellation, or criticism. Stand anyway. Truth never goes out of style. If you must choose between comfort and conviction, choose the cross. Faith forged in persecution will preach even after your voice is gone.

REFLECTIVE STANCE:

How is God calling me to stand firm when my faith is tested by criticism or conflict?

____

____

____

"Persecution proves purpose; pressure only polishes the diamond of faith."
— Rev. Unnia L. Pettus, Ph.D.

PRAYER:

Lord, thank You for trusting me with trials that testify. Give me courage to stand for truth without fear. Let Your Spirit strengthen my resolve to love those who oppose me. May my life reflect Your grace under pressure.
In Jesus's name, Amen.

MY FAITH NOTES FOR TODAY

____

____

____

MY FAITH DECLARATION:
I stand firm for Christ no matter the cost.

____

____

____

DAY 67
Faith That Finds Strength Again
— Isaiah 40:31 —
Renewed Like Eagles

"But He was wounded for our transgressions, He was bruised for our iniquities: the chastisement of our peace was upon Him; and with His stripes we are healed."
— Isaiah 53:5 (KJV)

DEVOTIONAL

Healing faith begins at the cross. Jesus didn't just die for sin; He carried sickness to the same tomb and left it there. Perfect faith clings to the promise that by His stripes, we are healed—present tense, permanent truth.

Sickness may touch the body, but it cannot infect the soul anchored in Christ. The woman with the issue of blood pressed through a crowd with desperation and declaration: "If I may but touch His garment, I shall be whole." Faith always finds a way to reach Him.

When the world says "incurable," heaven says "possible." God still heals through medicine, miracles, and moments of mercy. The method may differ, but the Healer remains the same.

Perfect faith doesn't ignore pain; it invites purpose into it. Paul's thorn reminded him that grace works where weakness stays. Sometimes God heals instantly; sometimes gradually; sometimes eternally—but always completely in His plan.

Speak life over your body daily. Declare, "It is well with my soul and my cells." Faith refuses to let diagnosis define destiny. The same Spirit that raised Jesus lives in you—resurrection power in every breath.

REFLECTIVE STANCE:

Where do I need to speak healing and hope over my life today?

____

____

____

"Faith doesn't deny symptoms; it declares sovereignty."
— Rev. Unnia L. Pettus, Ph.D.

PRAYER:

Father, thank You for being Jehovah Rapha, my Healer. I receive Your healing power in every part of my body and mind. Increase my faith to trust You beyond what I feel. Let Your stripes manifest wholeness in me today. In Jesus's name, Amen.

MY FAITH NOTES FOR TODAY

____

____

____

MY FAITH DECLARATION:

By His stripes I am healed and whole.

____

____

____

DAY 68
Faith That Reclaims Joy
— Nehemiah 8:10 —
The Joy of the Lord Is Our Strength

"But my God shall supply all your need according to His riches in glory by Christ Jesus."
— Philippians 4:19 (KJV)

DEVOTIONAL

Poverty isn't only financial—it's any area where lack tries to limit faith. Perfect faith believes God as Jehovah Jireh, the One who provides not according to our paycheck but His power.

Elijah watched God feed him through ravens, then through a widow with one last meal. Provision follows obedience. The oil never ran out because faith kept pouring.

Faith that overcomes poverty sees resources through heaven's economy. The boy's lunch of five loaves and two fish fed thousands because it was surrendered. What you give in faith multiplies beyond measure.

Perfect faith shifts language from scarcity to sufficiency. Instead of "I don't have enough," it declares, "God is enough." Gratitude opens the gate to abundance.

When faith leads finances, generosity flows. Giving becomes worship, not worry. Paul reminded the Philippians that their generosity triggered heaven's guarantee: "My God shall supply."

The Provider still performs today. Poverty bows where faith sows.

REFLECTIVE STANCE:
What area of lack is God inviting me to trust Him to supply?

____

____

____

"Faith turns lack into launch pads for God's limitless provision."
— Rev. Unnia L. Pettus, Ph.D.

PRAYER:
Lord, thank You for being my Provider. Shift my eyes from scarcity to sufficiency. Teach me to give cheerfully and expect abundantly. Every need is an opportunity to see Your hand. I trust You for overflow and wisdom.
In Jesus's name, Amen.

MY FAITH NOTES FOR TODAY

MY FAITH DECLARATION:

God is my Source; I shall not lack.

DAY 69
Faith That Speaks Victory
— 1 Corinthians 15:57 —
Christ's Triumph Over Death

"For a just man falleth seven times, and riseth up again."
— Proverbs 24:16 (KJV)

DEVOTIONAL

Failure doesn't define the faithful; it develops them. Peter denied Jesus three times but preached with power fifty days later. Perfect faith falls forward, not backward. Every fall is a classroom. When you learn, you win. God specializes in recycling failure into fuel. Jonah ran, sank, repented, and still fulfilled his call. Grace doesn't erase mistakes—it transforms them.

Faith that overcomes failure refuses condemnation. Romans 8:1 declares, "There is therefore now no condemnation to them which are in Christ Jesus." You can rise because mercy lifts you. Perfect faith also redefines success. It's not never falling—it's never quitting. Every stumble still ends in victory when surrender meets Savior.

David failed morally, yet wrote psalms that heal millions. The same God who forgave him forgives you. Failure may delay you, but it cannot disqualify what grace has appointed.

REFLECTIVE STANCE:
Where has God turned my failures into fresh faith?

____

____

____

"Failure is faith's fall that leads to a greater rise."

— Rev. Unnia L. Pettus, Ph.D.

PRAYER:
Father, thank You for mercy that lifts me after every fall. Forgive me for mistakes and remind me of Your grace. Strengthen me to rise again with wisdom and courage. Let my past become proof of Your power.
In Jesus's name, Amen.

MY FAITH NOTES FOR TODAY

____

____

____

MY FAITH DECLARATION:
I rise again by the grace of God.

____

____

____

DAY 70
Faith That Refuses Defeat
— Romans 8:37 —
More Than Conquerors
Through Christ

"Jesus said unto her, I am the resurrection, and the life: he that believeth in Me, though he were dead, yet shall he live."
— John 11 : 25 (KJV)

DEVOTIONAL

Death is life's loudest enemy, but perfect faith hears a louder voice—Resurrection. When Jesus stood at Lazarus's tomb, He didn't weep in defeat but in divine determination. He declared life into what others had buried.

Faith that overcomes death sees beyond the grave. Every ending becomes a new beginning in Christ. The cross looked final until the stone rolled away. Perfect faith doesn't deny grief; it defies despair. Paul called death "swallowed up in victory." When believers die, they don't disappear—they depart into glory. Faith faces mortality with immortality's mindset. To live is Christ; to die is gain. (Philippians 1:21)

Even before physical death, some things—dreams, confidence, hope—seem to die. Jesus still resurrects those, too. The same voice that said, "Lazarus, come forth," calls your faith to live again. Resurrection isn't just an event; it's a Person living in you.

REFLECTIVE STANCE:
What dream, hope, or relationship is God calling me to believe can live again?

____

____

____

"Resurrection faith believes God even at the grave."
— Rev. Unnia L. Pettus, Ph.D.

PRAYER:
*Lord, thank You for being Resurrection and Life.
Breathe new life into every area that has died in me.
Strengthen my hope and renew my joy. Remind me
that death never has the final word—You do.
In Jesus's name, Amen.*

MY FAITH NOTES FOR TODAY

____

____

____

MY FAITH DECLARATION:
Because He lives, I live and hope again.

____

____

____

Days 71 - 80
Faith That Sees the Impossible

DAY 71
Faith That Sees Beyond the Storm
— Mark 4:39 —
Jesus and the Disciples in the Boat

"And he arose, and rebuked the wind, and said unto the sea, Peace, be still. And the wind ceased, and there was a great calm."
— Mark 4:39 (KJV)

DEVOTIONAL

Faith that sees beyond the storm looks past the thunder to the testimony. The disciples panicked when waves crashed over their boat, but Jesus slept in peace. Perfect faith knows the difference between danger and destiny—storms may shake the boat, but they can't sink the Savior.

Every believer faces seasons when winds howl louder than hope. But storms reveal sovereignty. Jesus didn't just still the sea; He showed the disciples that peace travels with Him. When you walk with the Prince of Peace, you carry calm into chaos.

Faith that sees the impossible doesn't fixate on the size of the storm—it focuses on the strength of the Word. One command from Jesus—"Peace, be still"—transformed turmoil into tranquility. The same Word still speaks today when anxiety rises or circumstances rage.

Sometimes God calms the storm around you; other times He calms the storm within you. Either way, faith learns that silence from heaven is not absence but assurance. His quiet presence proves control.

Perfect faith rests while others run. It understands that God never abandons what He boards. If Jesus is in your boat, you can sleep through the storm too.

When life's waves overwhelm, remember the shore is already set. The same hand that rebukes wind also carries you forward.

REFLECTIVE STANCE:
What "storm" in my life do I need to surrender to Jesus' peace today?

____

____

____

"Faith doesn't wait for calm; it speaks calm into chaos."
— Rev. Unnia L. Pettus, Ph.D.

PRAYER:
Lord, thank You for commanding peace in every storm I face. Teach me to trust Your Word above the wind. Anchor my soul in Your presence until fear fades. Let Your calm flow through me to others.
In Jesus's name, Amen.

MY FAITH NOTES FOR TODAY

____

____

____

MY FAITH DECLARATION:
Peace is my portion because Jesus is in my boat.

____

____

____

DAY 72
Faith That Sees Open Doors
— Revelation 3:8 —
The Church of Philadelphia

"I know thy works: behold, I have set before thee an open door, and no man can shut it."
— Revelation 3:8 (KJV)

DEVOTIONAL

Faith that sees open doors discerns divine opportunity in ordinary moments. The church in Philadelphia had "little strength" but big faith; God promised no man could close what He had opened. Perfect faith doesn't chase doors—it trusts the Doorkeeper.

Many believers waste energy knocking on closed places. Faith learns to thank God for the "no," because it makes room for the "next." Closed doors protect purpose. The same God who opens paths through Red Seas also shuts lions' mouths in dens.

Faith that sees the impossible knows timing is everything. When Paul tried to preach in Asia, the Spirit forbade him; later, Macedonia opened. Delay isn't denial—it's direction. God's doors open when destiny aligns.

Perfect faith keeps moving even when hinges creak slowly. Patience prepares possession. Don't push; pray. The key of David—Christ Himself—unlocks what persistence alone cannot. When God opens a door, expect opposition. Every opportunity draws resistance, but no force can cancel favor. Walk boldly through what He has prepared.

Doors aren't just physical—they're spiritual invitations. Step through with gratitude and expectation.

REFLECTIVE STANCE:

Where is God inviting me to walk boldly through an open door today?

____

____

____

"When faith turns the handle, destiny opens wide."

— Rev. Unnia L. Pettus, Ph.D.

PRAYER:

Father, thank You for every door You've opened and every one You've closed. Sharpen my discernment to recognize Your timing. Give me courage to walk where You lead and peace to wait when You say still. In Jesus's name, Amen.

MY FAITH NOTES FOR TODAY

MY FAITH DECLARATION:
Every door God opens, I will enter with courage.

DAY 73
Faith That Sees Miracles in Motion
— John 2:1–11 —
Wedding at Cana of Galilee

"Behold, I will do a new thing; now it shall spring forth; shall ye not know it? I will even make a way in the wilderness, and rivers in the desert."
— Isaiah 43:19 (KJV)

DEVOTIONAL

Faith that sees provision in dry places recognizes that scarcity never limits God. Israel wandered forty years, yet manna fell daily. Perfect faith learns to look for miracles in monotonous places. Sometimes deserts are divine classrooms. God uses dryness to teach dependence. When resources run out, revelation runs over. Faith sees the hand of God where others see hopeless ground.

Elijah's brook dried up, but the Word of the Lord never did. A widow's jar looked empty until obedience poured abundance. Provision often hides behind obedience. Perfect faith refuses panic when the landscape looks lifeless. The same God who sent water from a rock can send rivers through your wilderness. Your drought may be the setup for a downpour.

Faith that sees the impossible praises before provision arrives. Gratitude attracts glory. Speak streams into sight. Declare, "God is doing a new thing!" When life feels barren, remember: deserts bloom when faith believes.

REFLECTIVE STANCE:

Where do I need to expect new provision in a "dry" season?

____

____

____

"Faith finds rivers where others see sand."
— Rev. Unnia L. Pettus, Ph.D.

PRAYER:

Lord, thank You for being my Source in every season. Teach me to trust Your provision even when I can't predict it. Make my desert fruitful with faith. Let miracles spring forth in unexpected places.
In Jesus's name, Amen.

MY FAITH NOTES FOR TODAY

____

____

____

MY FAITH DECLARATION:
My wilderness will bloom with God's provision.

____

____

____

Day 74
Faith That Sees Purpose in Pain
— Genesis 50:20 —
Joseph's Testimony of God's Goodness

"For the battle is not yours, but God's."
— 2 Chronicles 20:15 (KJV)

DEVOTIONAL

Before Jehoshaphat lifted a sword, he lifted a song. Perfect faith sees victory before the battle begins because it knows who truly fights. Worship was Judah's weapon, and praise became their power.

Faith that sees the impossible doesn't wait for evidence; it stands on expectancy. When armies gather, and odds stack high, faith remembers that heaven never loses.

Perfect faith positions itself in praise. Jehoshaphat sent singers ahead of soldiers. Their melody moved mountains faster than military might. Worship still wins wars today—it shifts focus from threat to throne.

Faith also listens for instruction before acting. God told Judah where to stand and when to move.

Strategy follows surrender. Even when you feel surrounded, faith sees angels already stationed on your side. God's glory always outnumbers the enemy's army.

Victory is not about strength but surrender. When you hand the battle to God, you've already won.

REFLECTIVE STANCE:
What battle must I hand over to God completely today?

____

____

____

"Faith doesn't fight for victory—it fights from victory."

— Rev. Unnia L. Pettus, Ph.D.

PRAYER:
Lord, thank You that every battle belongs to You. Teach me to praise before I see results. Strengthen my trust when the enemy surrounds me. Let my worship be warfare and my confidence rest in You.
In Jesus's name, Amen.

MY FAITH NOTES FOR TODAY

MY FAITH DECLARATION:

The battle is God's, and victory is mine through Him.

DAY 75
Faith That Sees God in the Valley
— Psalm 23:4 —
David in the Shadow of Death

"And I will restore to you the years that the locust hath eaten."
— Joel 2:25 (KJV)

DEVOTIONAL

Faith that sees restoration believes nothing is too lost for God to rebuild. Israel's fields were ravaged, but God promised to redeem their years. Perfect faith looks at ruin and still expects rain.

Restoration isn't just return—it's renewal. God doesn't give back what you had; He gives better. Job lost everything, yet received double when he prayed for his friends.

Faith that sees the impossible understands timing. Years may seem wasted, but heaven redeems moments. Every tear watered a harvest you haven't seen yet.

Perfect faith forgives what was stolen and focuses on what's still promised. Restoration begins when resentment ends. When locusts devour, God delivers. He restores peace, purpose, and plenty. Your past pain is soil for future growth.

Declare this truth: "Nothing lost will stay lost in God's hands."

REFLECTIVE STANCE:
What area of my life do I need to believe God can restore?

____

____

____

"Faith doesn't just recover—it rebuilds."
— Rev. Unnia L. Pettus, Ph.D.

PRAYER:
Father, thank You for being the God of restoration.
Renew my hope for every area that seems ruined.
Replace loss with life and mourning with miracles.
Restore my joy and multiply my testimony.
In Jesus's name, Amen.

MY FAITH NOTES FOR TODAY

____

____

____

MY FAITH DECLARATION:
God restores everything the enemy tried to destroy.

____

____

____

DAY 76
Faith That Sees Promise in the Process
— Romans 8:28 —
Paul on Divine Purpose

"But they that wait upon the Lord shall renew their strength; they shall mount up with wings as eagles; they shall run, and not be weary; and they shall walk, and not faint."
— Isaiah 40:31 (KJV)

DEVOTIONAL

Faith that sees victory in waiting learns that delay is never denial. The waiting room of God is where wings are built. Those who rush may run, but only those who wait soar. The Hebrew word for wait (qavah) means to bind together — to twist like cords. Waiting doesn't weaken faith; it intertwines it with God's will.

Abraham waited twenty-five years for Isaac. Joseph waited thirteen years in prison. David waited decades to wear the crown already promised. Waiting seasons refine character before revealing crowns. Perfect faith trusts God's pace even when the promise feels postponed.

The enemy whispers, "Nothing's happening," but heaven is preparing. Waiting activates unseen work. While Sarah's womb was silent, God was shaping nations within it. While Joseph sat in prison, He positioned Pharaoh's dream. Faith sees what patience conceives.

When you feel weary, remember the eagle. It doesn't fight the storm; it rides it higher. Waiting isn't wasted when it's worshipful. Those who serve while they wait soar stronger.

Faith that sees victory in waiting doesn't complain — it communes. It turns delay into devotion. Every moment teaches reliance, humility, and endurance.

Perfect faith says, "Even if it takes longer, I still believe." The promise is sure because the Promiser cannot lie.

REFLECTIVE STANCE:

Where might God be strengthening me through waiting?

____

____

____

"Waiting is the womb where winning faith is born."

— Rev. Unnia L. Pettus, Ph.D.

PRAYER:
Lord, thank You for reminding me that waiting seasons are working seasons. Teach me to serve, trust, and worship while I wait. Renew my strength until I rise above weariness. Let my patience produce power. In Jesus's name, Amen.

MY FAITH NOTES FOR TODAY

____

____

____

MY FAITH DECLARATION:
I wait with worship and soar with strength.

____

____

____

DAY 77
Faith That Sees Beyond the Cross
— Luke 24:6–7 —
Jesus' Resurrection Revealed

"Who hath despised the day of small things?"
— Zechariah 4:10 (KJV)

DEVOTIONAL

Faith that sees the impossible begins by recognizing God in the insignificant. Zechariah reminded Israel not to despise the day of small beginnings because the same God who starts small finishes strong.

Perfect faith celebrates progress, not perfection. David's training ground was not a palace but a pasture. Before he faced Goliath, he faced a lion and a bear. Each small victory built confidence for greater glory. When Elijah's servant saw a cloud the size of a man's hand, Elijah saw a storm. Faith interprets small signs as large confirmations. Little beginnings carry big potential when touched by heaven.

God hides miracles in mundane moments. The widow's oil looked like "just a jar," but when poured in faith, it paid debts and secured destiny. Faith that honors small things will always see big outcomes. Perfect faith recognizes that size never limits significance. The mustard seed is tiny yet moves mountains. God delights in multiplying what others overlook.

Today, thank Him for small mercies — a sunrise, a breath, a smile, a seed of hope. What starts small can end supernatural.

REFLECTIVE STANCE:
What small beginning in my life do I need to celebrate as sacred?

____

____

____

"Small steps of faith lead to giant leaps of destiny."
— Rev. Unnia L. Pettus, Ph.D.

PRAYER:
Father, thank You for using small things to show great power. Open my eyes to see Your hand in humble beginnings. Bless my obedience in the ordinary so it produces extraordinary outcomes.
In Jesus's name, Amen.

MY FAITH NOTES FOR TODAY

____

____

____

MY FAITH DECLARATION:
I honor small starts because God multiplies my faith.

____

____

____

DAY 78
Faith That Sees Family Restored
— Luke 15:20 —
The Prodigal Son and the Father's Embrace

"And we know that all things work together for good to them that love God, to them who are the called according to His purpose."
— Romans 8:28 (KJV)

DEVOTIONAL

Faith that sees purpose in pain refuses to let suffering silence belief. Pain may feel pointless until faith translates it into purpose. Joseph's betrayal became Egypt's salvation; his dungeon became destiny's doorway.

Perfect faith redefines pain as preparation. God never wastes wounds. What breaks you today may bless others tomorrow. Every tear is testimony fertilizer.

When Paul's thorn pierced his flesh, grace anchored his heart. He learned that weakness attracts divine strength. Faith doesn't deny discomfort — it discovers design within it. Jesus turned crucifixion into resurrection. The nails that looked like defeat became redemption's keys. If Calvary carried purpose, so does your cross.

Faith that sees purpose in pain keeps perspective: suffering is temporary, but glory is eternal. The Spirit intercedes with groanings too deep for words — meaning heaven feels your hurt.

Perfect faith says, "This hurts, but it's holy." Brokenness births beauty when placed in God's hands.

REFLECTIVE STANCE:

What pain might God be using to shape my purpose?

____

____

____

"Pain becomes purpose when surrendered to the Potter's hand."

— Rev. Unnia L. Pettus, Ph.D.

Prayer:
Lord, thank You for redeeming every ache for Your glory. Help me trust Your plan even when I don't understand. Turn my wounds into worship and my tears into testimony.
In Jesus's name, Amen.

MY FAITH NOTES FOR TODAY

____

____

____

MY FAITH DECLARATION:
My pain has purpose because God is in control.

____

____

____

DAY 79
Faith That Sees God's Hand
— Exodus 14:31 —
Israel Delivered at the Red Sea

"The light shineth in darkness; and the darkness comprehended it not."
— John 1:5 (KJV)

DEVOTIONAL

Faith that sees light in darkness remembers that dawn always follows night. Darkness may cover the earth, but it can't cancel the light God planted within you.

When the world feels dim, faith becomes the lamp. The psalmist wrote, "Thy word is a lamp unto my feet." Perfect faith walks one step at a time, trusting revelation over visibility.

In Egypt's plagues, Israel had light in Goshen while others stumbled. Divine distinction glows brightest in gloom. Faith sees that even shadows require light's presence.

Jesus is the Light of the world, yet darkness crucified Him. But three days later, light walked out of a tomb. Resurrection proves that darkness always loses the debate.

When despair whispers, "This is the end," faith replies, "It's just midnight — morning's on the way." Perfect faith keeps its lamp trimmed, filled with oil of expectation.

Today, shine by believing. You carry divine illumination. Your faith can light another's path.

REFLECTIVE STANCE:
Where is God calling me to shine even when life feels dark?

____

____

____

"Darkness cannot drown a believer who carries divine light."
— Rev. Unnia L. Pettus, Ph.D.

PRAYER:
Father, thank You for being my Light in every dark place. Help me to see Your glory when life grows dim. Let my faith reflect Your brilliance and draw others to hope.
In Jesus's name, Amen.

MY FAITH NOTES FOR TODAY

____

____

____

MY FAITH DECLARATION:

The light of Christ shines through me no matter the darkness.

____

____

____

DAY 80
Faith That Sees the Crown Ahead
— 2 Timothy 4:8 —
Paul's Reward for Finishing the Race

"While we look not at the things which are seen, but at the things which are not seen: for the things which are seen are temporal; but the things which are not seen are eternal."
— 2 Corinthians 4:18 (KJV)

DEVOTIONAL

Faith that sees the unseen lifts eyes above circumstances. The visible world deceives; the invisible defines destiny. Perfect faith perceives eternal realities beyond temporary trouble.

Elisha's servant panicked at an encircling army until the prophet prayed, "Lord, open his eyes." Suddenly he saw horses and chariots of fire. The same God who surrounded them still surrounds you. Faith looks through heaven's lens. It sees angels where fear sees enemies, provision where worry sees lack, victory where vision once saw defeat. Moses endured Egypt "as seeing Him who is invisible." He kept focus on the eternal even when Pharaoh's rage burned. Faith chooses the unseen because it trusts the Unseen Hand.

Perfect faith trains spiritual sight through Scripture and prayer. The more you know His Word, the clearer your vision becomes.

When you see the unseen, you stop living by reaction and start walking by revelation. Every trial becomes transparent to purpose.

REFLECTIVE STANCE:

How can I shift my focus from what I see to what God says?

____

____

____

"Faith sees with heaven's eyes when sight fails on earth."

— Rev. Unnia L. Pettus, Ph.D.

PRAYER:

Lord, thank You for opening my spiritual eyes. Help me look beyond what's visible to trust what's eternal. Strengthen my vision to see Your presence in every place.
In Jesus's name, Amen.

MY FAITH NOTES FOR TODAY

____

____

____

MY FAITH DECLARATION:
I walk by faith, not by sight, seeing the unseen.

____

____

____

Days 81 ~ 90
Faith That Stands

DAY 81
Faith That Stands on His Word
— Matthew 4:4 —
Jesus in the Wilderness Temptation

"Death and life are in the power of the tongue: and they that love it shall eat the fruit thereof."
— Proverbs 18:21 (KJV)

DEVOTIONAL

Faith that speaks life understands that every word plants either life or loss. The tongue is not a toy—it's a tool for transformation. God spoke the world into being, and He invites believers to mirror that creative authority. Perfect faith refuses to echo fear; it declares God's Word until atmosphere and attitude align with heaven's truth.

Israel's future often rose or fell with its confession. Ten spies said, "We be not able," while Joshua and Caleb declared, "We are well able." The difference wasn't strength but speech. What you say shapes what you see.

Jesus called Lazarus forth with words. The grave obeyed the gospel sound. Your declaration carries resurrection potential too. When despair tempts silence, speak Scripture instead: "I shall not die, but live, and declare the works of the Lord." (Psalm 118:17)

Faith-filled language rewires the mind. Speak blessings over brokenness. Replace "I can't" with "God can." What you continually confess, you eventually create.

Perfect faith doesn't ignore reality; it invites divinity into it. Speaking life is not denial—it's direction. It steers the soul toward victory.

Today, choose speech that summons strength. Let gratitude guard your mouth and grace govern your tone.

REFLECTIVE STANCE:

What words have I spoken that I need to replace with faith?

____

____

____

"When your words agree with God's Word, miracles manifest."

— Rev. Unnia L. Pettus, Ph.D.

PRAYER:
Lord, purify my tongue. Let every word build and bless. Teach me to speak life when negativity whispers. Fill my mouth with truth, hope, and praise. May my language mirror Your love.
In Jesus's name, Amen.

MY FAITH NOTES FOR TODAY

____

____

____

MY FAITH DECLARATION:

I speak life, and life answers back.

____

____

____

DAY 82
Faith That Stands Firm in Battle
— Ephesians 6:13 —
Armor of God for Every Believer

"He sent his word, and healed them, and delivered them from their destructions."
— Psalm 107:20 (KJV)

DEVOTIONAL

Faith that speaks healing believes the Word carries power to cure. God's promises are prescriptions for the soul. When pain persists, proclaim the Word louder than the wound. The centurion told Jesus, "Speak the word only, and my servant shall be healed." Faith never needs proof; it trusts the potency of divine utterance. One sentence from the Savior silenced sickness instantly.

Healing begins in hearing. Romans 10:17 says, "Faith cometh by hearing, and hearing by the word of God." Speak Scripture aloud until it saturates your spirit. Every declaration disinfects doubt. Jesus healed ten lepers, but only one returned with gratitude. Gratitude keeps healing whole. Thanking God in advance activates recovery before results appear.

Perfect faith speaks healing even while symptoms shout otherwise. It calls things that be not as though they were. Let your vocabulary become victory. Whisper verses in waiting rooms, sing them through surgery, declare them during discouragement. God's Word never fails.

REFLECTIVE STANCE:
Where do I need to speak God's healing Word over my life?

____

____

____

"Your mouth can be medicine when filled with God's Word."

— Rev. Unnia L. Pettus, Ph.D.

PRAYER:
*Healer, send Your Word again. Restore what illness tried to steal. Strengthen my faith to speak wholeness daily. Let every cell respond to heaven's command. I receive healing for body, mind, and spirit.
In Jesus's name, Amen.*

MY FAITH NOTES FOR TODAY

____

____

____

MY FAITH DECLARATION:

God's Word heals me from the inside out.

____

____

____

DAY 83
Faith That Stands When Tired
— Galatians 6:9 —
Paul's Encouragement to Not Grow Weary

"Have not I commanded thee? Be strong and of a good courage; be not afraid, neither be thou dismayed: for the Lord thy God is with thee whithersoever thou goest."
— Joshua 1:9 (KJV)

DEVOTIONAL

Faith that speaks courage confronts fear with confession. God told Joshua three times to be strong before he ever swung a sword. Words build warriors. Courage isn't absence of fear—it's presence of faith. David declared victory long before Goliath fell. He said, "This day will the Lord deliver thee into mine hand." His mouth marched before his feet.

Perfect faith rehearses God's record instead of reasons to retreat. Every "I am with you" from Scripture still echoes through storms. Speak courage when confidence feels crushed. Tell your soul, "God is for me." Remind fear it has an eviction notice.

Faith that speaks courage also speaks community. Encourage others aloud. Courage multiplies when spoken collectively. Every believer is one brave confession away from breakthrough. Say what God says until strength returns.

REFLECTIVE STANCE:
What fear do I need to silence with courage-filled words today?

____

____

____

"Courage is faith finding its voice."
— Rev. Unnia L. Pettus, Ph.D.

PRAYER:
Lord, speak boldness into my heart. Remind me You go before me. Replace trembling with trust and panic with peace. Let my words reflect Your strength.
In Jesus's name, Amen.

MY FAITH NOTES FOR TODAY

____

____

____

MY FAITH DECLARATION:
I am strong, courageous, and confident in Christ.

____

____

____

DAY 84
Faith That Stands Against Giants
— 1 Samuel 17:45 —
David Confronts Goliath

"But my God shall supply all your need according to his riches in glory by Christ Jesus."
— Philippians 4:19 (KJV)

DEVOTIONAL

Faith that speaks provision calls abundance out of apparent lack. Paul wrote those words from prison, proving provision isn't limited by place. Perfect faith remembers that God is Jehovah-Jireh—the Lord who provides. Abraham spoke faith when Isaac asked, "Where is the lamb?" He answered, "God will provide Himself a lamb." His words pulled future grace into present need.

Provision often starts as declaration. The widow in 2 Kings 4 spoke obedience when told to borrow vessels. Her little oil flowed until no jars remained. What you declare determines how long the oil pours.

Faith speaks gratitude before goods arrive. Say "Thank You" while the shelf looks empty. Thanksgiving multiplies resources. Jesus blessed five loaves and two fish—and thousands ate.

Perfect faith refuses scarcity thinking. You serve an unlimited Supplier. Speak supply, not shortage.

Today, let your mouth match God's might. Say, "I have everything I need for what God has called me to do."

REFLECTIVE STANCE:
Where do I need to speak God's provision into my life today?

____

____

____

"Provision begins with proclamation."
— Rev. Unnia L. Pettus, Ph.D.

PRAYER:
Provider, I trust Your endless supply. Open my eyes to see abundance where I saw lack. Multiply resources, favor, and faith. Let contentment and confidence replace worry.
In Jesus's name, Amen.

MY FAITH NOTES FOR TODAY

____

____

____

MY FAITH DECLARATION:
God meets my every need in overflowing measure.

____

____

____

DAY 85 Faith That Stands for Justice
— Numbers 27:1–11 —
Daughters of Zelophehad Seek Their Inheritance

"Thanks be to God, which giveth us the victory through our Lord Jesus Christ."
— 1 Corinthians 15:57 (KJV)

DEVOTIONAL

Faith that speaks victory declares triumph before the trumpet sounds. Paul wrote these words in a chapter about death, proving faith's vocabulary never changes—even at gravesides.

Victory speech shifts atmosphere. Israel shouted before Jericho's walls fell. Their praise became demolition. Sometimes faith's loudest weapon is worship. Perfect faith speaks victory through vision. It imagines the finish line even while fighting fatigue. Words shape endurance.

Jesus spoke victory from the cross: "It is finished." He wasn't announcing defeat—He was declaring dominion. Every believer carries that same triumphant tongue. Say, "I win in Christ," until your heart believes it. Confession creates confidence. Faith that speaks victory sees every battle as proof of blessing. If the fight is fierce, the future is fruitful.

REFLECTIVE STANCE:
Where is God calling me to proclaim victory even before I see it?

____

____

____

"Victory is voiced before it's visible."
— Rev. Unnia L. Pettus, Ph.D.

PRAYER:
Lord, thank You for making me more than a conqueror. Teach me to speak victory in valleys and on mountaintops. Let my words echo Your triumph. I walk in confidence today knowing the battle is already won. In Jesus's name, Amen.

MY FAITH NOTES FOR TODAY

____

____

____

MY FAITH DECLARATION:
I speak victory because Christ has already won.

____

____

____

DAY 86
Faith That Stands in Grace
— Romans 5:2 —
Paul on the Power of Grace

"The righteous cry, and the Lord heareth, and delivereth them out of all their troubles."
— Psalm 34:17 (KJV)

DEVOTIONAL

Faith that speaks deliverance learns that freedom begins with a cry. David wrote this psalm after escaping danger, proving that pain can still praise. Perfect faith doesn't hide its hurt—it calls heaven for help. Every cry of faith carries authority because it is aimed toward the Almighty.

When Israel groaned under Pharaoh, God heard and remembered His covenant. Deliverance always begins when faith opens its mouth. Your cry becomes the key that unlocks chains. Perfect faith declares deliverance before doors swing open. Paul and Silas prayed and sang in prison; praise shook foundations and released freedom. Their song became a sermon for the jailer. When you speak victory in confinement, chains can't stay closed.

Faith that speaks deliverance refuses despair. The righteous cry, and God delivers—not from some troubles but all of them. Speak that promise until it silences panic. Sometimes deliverance is external—God changes circumstance; sometimes it's internal—He changes your mind about it. Either way, your declaration invites divine movement.

Today, declare aloud, "The Lord is delivering me." Say it until peace replaces panic.

REFLECTIVE STANCE:

Where do I need to open my mouth and declare my deliverance?

____

____

____

"Deliverance begins the moment faith dares to speak."

— Rev. Unnia L. Pettus, Ph.D.

PRAYER:

Lord, thank You for hearing every cry of my heart. Break chains of fear and free me from every prison of the past. Let my voice become an instrument of victory. Teach me to speak freedom with confidence.
In Jesus's name, Amen.

MY FAITH NOTES FOR TODAY

MY FAITH DECLARATION:
I am delivered because the Lord hears me.

DAY 87
Faith That Stands in the Fire
— Daniel 3:25 —
The Fourth Man in the Furnace

"Weeping may endure for a night, but joy cometh in the morning."
— Psalm 30:5 (KJV)

DEVOTIONAL

Faith that speaks joy learns that mourning has a morning. David knew nights of tears but trusted dawn to deliver delight. Perfect faith proclaims joy even while eyes still glisten. Joy is not emotion; it's evidence—proof that faith still functions. Paul sang in prison, showing that joy lives beyond walls. When faith speaks joy, sorrow loses authority.

Perfect faith rehearses God's record. Every past rescue becomes rehearsal for today's rejoicing. The same God who turned David's mourning into dancing can turn your heartbreak into hallelujah. Faith that speaks joy refuses to let grief define identity. Tears may fall, but trust stands tall. Declare, "My joy is not gone; it's growing." Joy doesn't depend on circumstances—it flows from Christ within.

Jesus endured the cross "for the joy set before Him." If He found joy in sacrifice, so can we find purpose in pain. When the night feels long, speak morning over it. The Word still works: joy comes in the morning.

REFLECTIVE STANCE:

What situation requires me to speak joy before I feel it?

____

____

____

"Joy is the sound faith makes in the dark."
— Rev. Unnia L. Pettus, Ph.D.

PRAYER:

Father, thank You for being my source of joy. Teach me to rejoice when life hurts and to sing when seasons sting. Let Your Spirit restore my gladness and guard my gratitude.
In Jesus's name, Amen.

MY FAITH NOTES FOR TODAY

____

____

____

MY FAITH DECLARATION:
My night is ending; joy is rising.

____

____

____

DAY 88
Faith That Stands on the Rock
— Matthew 7:24 —
Jesus' Parable of the Wise Builder

"Peace I leave with you, my peace I give unto you: not as the world giveth, give I unto you."
— John 14:27 (KJV)

DEVOTIONAL

Faith that speaks peace does not wait for calm; it calls it. Jesus gifted peace like a legacy to His disciples. That same inheritance is yours. Perfect faith understands peace isn't the absence of pressure—it's authority amid it. When storms rage, speak, "Peace, be still," as Jesus did. The same Spirit that silenced Galilee lives within you.

Fear feeds on silence, but faith speaks serenity. Declare peace over your home, health, and heart. Your voice carries the vibration of victory. Paul wrote from prison, "Be careful for nothing... and the peace of God... shall keep your hearts." Peace guards like soldiers at the gate of your mind. Speak it and stand still.

Perfect faith trains the tongue to pronounce peace before problems pause. Every declaration rewires the soul for rest. Today, breathe deeply, speak softly, and believe boldly: Peace is mine.

REFLECTIVE STANCE:
Where do I need to speak God's peace right now?

____

____

____

"Peace is the language faith speaks when fear loses signal."
— Rev. Unnia L. Pettus, Ph.D.

PRAYER:
Prince of Peace, settle my spirit and still my storm. Teach me to release control and rest in Your care. Let Your calm reign where chaos once ruled. In Jesus's name, Amen.

MY FAITH NOTES FOR TODAY

____

____

____

MY FAITH DECLARATION:
Peace speaks louder than panic in my life.

____

____

____

DAY 89
Faith That Stands in Praise
— 2 Chronicles 20:22 —
Judah Worships Through Warfare

"Jesus said unto her, I am the resurrection, and the life: he that believeth in me, though he were dead, yet shall he live."
— John 11 : 25 (KJV)

DEVOTIONAL

Faith that speaks resurrection believes endings can begin again. When Martha mourned Lazarus, Jesus announced life in the language of faith. Perfect faith never buries possibility.

Every believer faces tomb moments—dreams that seem dead, hopes wrapped in grave clothes. But the same voice that called Lazarus still calls your purpose. Say aloud, "Come forth!" over what feels finished.

Resurrection faith speaks revival, not regret. It refuses to let the scent of death stop expectation. Jesus delayed arrival so glory could develop. Delays don't deny destiny—they display divinity. Perfect faith remembers: life always answers when the Lord calls.

Your comeback is coded in your confession. Speak life until lethargy leaves.
The stone may look sealed, but heaven holds the key. Faith doesn't fear finality—it foresees fulfillment.

Today, declare that everything buried in discouragement will rise again.

REFLECTIVE STANCE:

What dream or hope do I need to call back to life by faith?

____

____

____

"Resurrection begins where faith refuses to give up."
— Rev. Unnia L. Pettus, Ph.D.

PRAYER:

Lord of Life, thank You for resurrection power. Breathe new strength into tired places and revive every buried promise. Let hope rise from the ashes and faith flourish again.
In Jesus's name, Amen.

MY FAITH NOTES FOR TODAY

____

____

____

MY FAITH DECLARATION:
What looked dead will live again through Christ.

____

____

____

DAY 90
Faith That Stands Victorious
— Revelation 12:11 —
Overcoming by the Blood and Testimony

"In every thing give thanks: for this is the will of God in Christ Jesus concerning you."
— 1 Thessalonians 5:18 (KJV)

DEVOTIONAL

Faith that speaks gratitude sees goodness even in grief. Paul didn't say for everything—he said in everything. Thanksgiving is a posture, not a product. Perfect faith keeps praise flowing when provision seems faint. When Jesus blessed the five loaves, He thanked God before the miracle. Gratitude precedes multiplication. Say "Thank You" first, and heaven fills your hands after.

Perfect faith makes thanksgiving a weapon. Complaining confuses courage; praise produces peace. Even in prison, Paul and Silas sang until the walls trembled. Thankful faith turns cells into sanctuaries. Speaking gratitude shifts atmosphere faster than anxiety can settle. The grateful heart becomes God's favorite dwelling place. When you can't trace His hand, thank Him for His heart. Gratitude opens gates that grief cannot guard. Psalm 100 declares, "Enter into his gates with thanksgiving." Your thank-you is the key to access. Today, declare, "I choose to be grateful no matter what I see."

REFLECTIVE STANCE:

Where can I practice gratitude before change appears?

____

____

____

"Gratitude is faith's proof that God has already been good."
— Rev. Unnia L. Pettus, Ph.D.

PRAYER:

Father, thank You for being faithful in all seasons. Teach me to speak thanksgiving when trouble tempts complaint. Let my praise rise higher than my pain. I thank You for what You've done, what You're doing, and what's still on the way.
In Jesus's name, Amen.

MY FAITH NOTES FOR TODAY

____

____

____

MY FAITH DECLARATION:
Gratitude is my daily language of faith.

____

____

____

Days 91 ~ 100
Faith That Finishes

DAY 91
Faith That Finishes the Race
— 2 Timothy 4:7 —
Paul on Fighting the Good Fight

"I have fought a good fight, I have finished my course, I have kept the faith."
— 2 Timothy 4:7 (KJV)

DEVOTIONAL

Faith that finishes strong refuses to fade when fatigue sets in. Paul's final words ring with triumph, not tears. He had endured beatings, betrayal, and burdens, yet still declared victory because he never abandoned belief. Perfect faith understands that finishing is greater than starting.

The Greek word for finished (teleō) means "to complete fully." It's the same word Jesus used on the cross—"It is finished." Completion is the crown of conviction. Faith that finishes strong doesn't need comfort—it draws courage from calling. Every trial trains endurance. Each disappointment disciplines dependence. When others quit, finishers worship. They know crowns await consistency. Heaven applauds those who keep going when applause on earth stops.

Perfect faith looks forward. Paul said, "Henceforth there is laid up for me a crown of righteousness." Future focus fuels present perseverance.

`Today, strengthen your stride. The same God who started you will sustain you.

REFLECTIVE STANCE:

Where is God asking me to finish what I started by faith?

____

____

____

"Finishing faith doesn't fizzle; it flourishes under fire."

— Rev. Unnia L. Pettus, Ph.D.

PRAYER:

Lord, thank You for giving me grace to endure. Remind me that completion honors You. Strengthen my resolve to finish every assignment well. Let perseverance perfect my purpose. In Jesus's name, Amen.

MY FAITH NOTES FOR TODAY

____

____

____

MY FAITH DECLARATION:
I will finish strong because faith fuels my endurance.

____

____

____

DAY 92
Faith That Fulfills the Promise
— Joshua 21:45 —
God's Word Never Fails

"There is therefore now no condemnation to them which are in Christ Jesus."
— Romans 8:1 (KJV)

DEVOTIONAL

Faith that finishes strong also forgives freely—including yourself. Many saints stay stuck in guilt while grace keeps calling. Condemnation cripples confidence, but Christ cancels it completely. Peter wept bitterly after denying Jesus, yet the risen Lord restored him. Self-forgiveness unlocks future faithfulness. You cannot finish strong dragging yesterday's shame. Perfect faith receives pardon personally. Grace is not generic—it has your name written in blood. The enemy loves replaying failure; faith presses "delete." Your mistakes are not your master. When Jesus said, "Go and sin no more," He gave both forgiveness and forward momentum. Release regret. Redeem time. Rejoice in mercy.

REFLECTIVE STANCE:
What guilt do I need to release so I can run freely?

____

____

____

"Faith forgives the self so the soul can soar again."
— Rev. Unnia L. Pettus, Ph.D.

PRAYER:
Lord, thank You for forgiving me completely. Help me extend that same grace inward. Silence shame and stir strength. Let Your mercy rewrite my memories. In Jesus's name, Amen.

MY FAITH NOTES FOR TODAY

____

____

____

MY FAITH DECLARATION:
I am free from condemnation and full of grace.

____

____

____

DAY 93
Faith That Rests in Peace
— Philippians 1:6 —
Paul's Confidence in God's Completion

"Let us not be weary in well doing: for in due season we shall reap, if we faint not."
— Galatians 6:9 (KJV)

DEVOTIONAL

Faith that finishes strong learns to outlast frustration. The road to reward runs through routine obedience. Noah built when there was no rain. His hammer became a hymn of hope. Perfect faith works while waiting. Weariness tempts you to quit right before the harvest. But God promises "due season." Delay is not denial—it's divine timing. Faith that stays the course keeps sowing kindness, prayer, and excellence even when unseen. Heaven tracks every seed. When you feel faint, remember Jesus carried His cross to completion. His perseverance purchased your promise. Perfect faith whispers, "I'll reap because I refused to retreat." Keep going.

REFLECTIVE STANCE:
Where is God calling me to keep sowing despite fatigue?

____

____

____

"Consistency is the quiet confession of lasting faith."

— Rev. Unnia L. Pettus, Ph.D.

PRAYER:
Father, renew my strength for daily obedience. Remind me that harvest follows hardship. Help me serve with joy and endure with hope.
In Jesus's name, Amen.

MY FAITH NOTES FOR TODAY

____

____

____

MY FAITH DECLARATION:
I will not faint; my season of reaping is near.

____

____

____

DAY 94
Faith That Gives Thanks Always
— 1 Thessalonians 5:18 —
Paul on Gratitude in Every Season

"And now abideth faith, hope, charity, these three; but the greatest of these is charity."
— 1 Corinthians 13:13 (KJV)

DEVOTIONAL

Faith that finishes strong must finish in love. Paul closed his masterpiece on gifts by crowning love supreme. Love is faith's final exam. Prophecies pass, tongues cease, but love lasts. Perfect faith proves itself through compassion, not comparison. Jesus washed feet before He wore a crown. Service is love's signature. Faith without love becomes noise. Love without faith becomes fear. Together, they reflect Christ completely. Endings test emotions. Choose tenderness over tension. The mark of mature faith is mercy. Let your legacy be love—acts of kindness, forgiveness, and generosity. That's finishing God's way.

REFLECTIVE STANCE:
Who needs to feel the love of Christ through me today?

____

____

____

"Faith may move mountains, but love moves hearts."

— Rev. Unnia L. Pettus, Ph.D.

PRAYER:
Lord, teach me to love deeply and serve joyfully. Let compassion crown my faith. Make me a channel of Your grace wherever I go.
In Jesus's name, Amen.

MY FAITH NOTES FOR TODAY

____

____

____

MY FAITH DECLARATION:
I finish every assignment in love.

____

____

____

DAY 95
Faith That Shines in Darkness
— Matthew 5:16 —
Jesus Calls Us the Light of the World

"Let every thing that hath breath praise the Lord. Praise ye the Lord."
— Psalm 150:6 (KJV)

DEVOTIONAL

The finale of faith is worship. When words fail, worship finishes sentences. Perfect faith ends not in complaint but in celebration. Job lost everything yet bowed, saying, "Blessed be the name of the Lord." True faith praises when life hurts. Worship refocuses vision. It shifts eyes from loss to Lordship. Each hallelujah rebuilds hope. Perfect faith realizes breath itself is borrowed mercy. Every inhale deserves a thank-You. Heaven's anthem echoes through earth's altars when believers praise through pain. Worship is how warriors rest. It's surrender wrapped in song.

REFLECTIVE STANCE:

Where can I replace worry with worship today?

____

____

____

"Worship is the finish line of faithful hearts."
— Rev. Unnia L. Pettus, Ph.D.

PRAYER:

Lord, receive my praise as proof of trust. Teach me to worship beyond emotion and circumstance. Let gratitude guard my heart every day.
In Jesus's name, Amen.

MY FAITH NOTES FOR TODAY

____

____

____

MY FAITH DECLARATION:

I will worship my way to the finish line.

____

____

____

DAY 96
Faith That Loves Like Christ
— John 13:34–35 —
Jesus' Command to Love One Another

"Nay, in all these things we are more than conquerors through him that loved us."
— Romans 8:37 (KJV)

DEVOTIONAL

Faith that finishes strong doesn't just survive—it supersedes. Paul listed tribulation, distress, peril, sword, and still shouted, "More than conquerors." Perfect faith celebrates while still bleeding. To be "more than conqueror" means the victory was guaranteed before the fight. The cross settled every conflict. Faith that finishes in victory stands when others sit in sorrow. It refuses defeat because Christ's resurrection rewrote the ending. Your scars are symbols of survival. What the enemy used to wound, God now uses to witness. Perfect faith finishes shouting, "I win through Him who loves me."

REFLECTIVE STANCE:
What victory must I claim again today by faith?

____

____

____

"Faith doesn't fight for victory — it finishes from it."

— Rev. Unnia L. Pettus, Ph.D.

PRAYER:
*Lord, thank You for victory through Your love.
Strengthen my spirit to stand in triumph. Let my life
testify that You always cause me to overcome.
In Jesus's name, Amen.*

MY FAITH NOTES FOR TODAY

____

____

____

MY FAITH DECLARATION:
I finish every fight already victorious in Christ.

____

____

____

DAY 97
Faith That Serves with Joy
— Colossians 3:23 —
Work as Unto the Lord

"My grace is sufficient for thee: for my strength is made perfect in weakness."
— 2 Corinthians 12:9 (KJV)

DEVOTIONAL

Perfect faith bows before perfect grace. Paul begged for thorn removal, but God offered sustaining strength. Sometimes grace doesn't take away—it takes over.

Faith that finishes in grace knows weakness is not wasted; it's where wonder works. Grace keeps you when grit can't. It's the glue of every testimony. When you can't see a way, grace whispers, "Still enough." Perfect faith ends every sentence with grace. From start to finish, grace writes the story.

REFLECTIVE STANCE:

Where is grace carrying me when strength runs out?

____

____

____

"Grace is the ground faith finishes on."
— Rev. Unnia L. Pettus, Ph.D.

PRAYER:
Lord, thank You for grace that never quits. Teach me to rest in Your sufficiency. Let weakness showcase Your strength.
In Jesus's name, Amen.

MY FAITH NOTES FOR TODAY

____

____

____

MY FAITH DECLARATION:
Grace is my finish line and my foundation.

____

____

____

DAY 98
Faith That Hopes Until the End
— Hebrews 10:23 —
Hold Fast Without Wavering

"Now the God of hope fill you with all joy and peace in believing."
— Romans 15:13 (KJV)

DEVOTIONAL

Faith that finishes strong ends in hope unshakable. Hope is faith's horizon—it keeps eyes lifted.

Abraham hoped against hope, believing in barren seasons. That hope birthed nations.

Perfect faith holds on when headlines hurt and hearts grow heavy. Hope anchors souls in storms.

Let God fill you again—with joy, peace, and believing.

Even on life's last day, hope whispers, "Heaven is home."

REFLECTIVE STANCE:
Where must I let hope refill what fear drained?

____

____

____

"Hope is faith's final heartbeat."
— Rev. Unnia L. Pettus, Ph.D.

PRAYER:
Lord, breathe fresh hope into weary places. Remind me that every ending is a beginning with You. Let joy and peace overflow as I believe.
In Jesus's name, Amen.

MY FAITH NOTES FOR TODAY

____

____

____

MY FAITH DECLARATION:
Hope anchors my heart in every storm.

____

____

____

DAY 99
Faith That Believes It Is Finished
— John 19:30 —
Jesus Declares the Victory Complete

"Looking unto Jesus the author and finisher of our faith."
— Hebrews 12:2 (KJV)

DEVOTIONAL

Every journey of faith ends where it began—at the cross. Jesus authored salvation with love and finished it with blood.

Perfect faith keeps its eyes on Him, not hurdles. The cross proves completion before coronation.

When you're weary, look up. Every drop of Calvary's crimson whispers, "It is finished."

Faith that finishes at the cross finds power to keep carrying it.

REFLECTIVE STANCE:
How can I refocus my faith on Jesus today?

____

____

____

"The finish line of faith runs through the cross."

— Rev. Unnia L. Pettus, Ph.D.

PRAYER:
Jesus, thank You for finishing what I could never start.
Keep me near Your cross until my heart mirrors Yours.
Let gratitude guide every step.
In Your name, Amen.

MY FAITH NOTES FOR TODAY

____

____

____

MY FAITH DECLARATION:
My faith begins and ends at the cross.

____

____

____

DAY 100
Faith That Celebrates the Victory
— Revelation 21:4 —
Heaven's Promise Fulfilled

"Well done, thou good and faithful servant... enter thou into the joy of thy lord."
— Matthew 25:21 (KJV)

DEVOTIONAL

The journey ends in joy. Heaven's words, "Well done," are faith's eternal echo. Perfect faith finishes with fulfillment because it followed faithfully.

All obedience leads home. Every unseen sacrifice sings here.

Faith that finishes forever sees reward not in riches but in relationship—entering the Lord's joy.

Perfect faith lives ready, serves willingly, and dies rejoicing.

May your legacy shout: "She believed, spoke, and watched God do it."

REFLECTIVE STANCE:
What will my "well done" sound like in eternity?

"Heaven's applause awaits the faithful finisher."
— Rev. Unnia L. Pettus, Ph.D.

PRAYER:
Father, thank You for the privilege of faith that endures to eternity. Help me live worthy of Your "well done." Let my final breath be full of praise.
In Jesus's name, Amen.

MY FAITH NOTES FOR TODAY

MY FAITH DECLARATION:
I will finish faithfully and forever with joy.

About The Author
Rev. Dr. Unnia L. Pettus, Ph.D

Rev. Dr. Unnia L. Pettus, Ph.D., is an ordained ministry leader, best-selling author, adjunct faculty member, and publicist. She is the

DR. UNNIA L. PETTUS, PH.D.

Founder and CEO of Nobody But God Ministries and Pettus PR based in Washington, D.C.

Licensed to preach the gospel in October 1998, she made history as the first woman to be licensed at East Friendship Baptist Church in its 58 years of ministry. She was ordained in 2003 and founded Nobody But God Ministries in 2007.

Dr. Pettus holds a B.A. (Broadcast Journalism, Summa Cum Laude) from Howard University (1990), an M.A. (Public Communications, Summa Cum Laude) from American University (1995), and a Ph.D. (Mass Communications) from the University of Maryland at College Park (2003), with doctoral cognate work at Howard University School of Divinity.

A four-time cancer survivor (colon, uterine, kidney, and breast), a stroke survivor with right-side paralysis, and a domestic violence survivor, she has become a powerful voice of hope and advocacy. She holds the 2023 Presidential Lifetime Achievement Award for her documented volunteer service of over 4,000 hours in health, ministry, and community work.

Dr. Pettus has served as a tenure-track Assistant Professor of Mass Communications at Bowie State University and as adjunct faculty teaching undergraduate and graduate courses in PR, marketing, and entrepreneurship at Howard University for more than a decade. She has also taught graduate master of

Business Administration (M.B.A.) courses at Strayer University.

She is the author of Nobody But God: A Journey of Faith from Tears to Triumph (2007) and co-author of several Amazon best-selling devotional books. She serves as a motivational speaker, an award-winning health equity advocate for cancer and heart disease patients and survivors like herself, and a faith and life coach to individuals overcoming adversity and stepping into their purpose.

Her life mantra is that "it is not what happens to you but how you respond to it that matters the most!" She chooses to "walk by faith, not by sight" (2 Corinthians 5:7) — and through this devotional, she invites you to do the same.

9 798993 971209